TRAVELER'S GUIDE
To Major U.S. Airports

Richard Barbare
Linda Hafendorfer

Peachtree Publishers, Ltd.
Atlanta • Memphis

While every care has been taken to assure the accuracy of the information in this guide, the passage of time will always bring change, and consequently the publisher cannot accept responsibility for errors that may occur. All information is based on that available at press time; the prudent traveler will avoid inconvenience by calling ahead.

Published by
Peachtree Publishers, Ltd.
494 Armour Circle, N.E.
Atlanta, Georgia 30324

Manufactured in the United States of America

10 9 8 7 6 5 4 3 2 1

Design by Patricia Joe

Library of Congress Catalog Card Number 89-060907

ISBN 0-934601-70-4

ACKNOWLEDGMENT

Our special thanks to family and friends for their encouragement and support, and to the behind-the-scenes airport personnel who contributed their time and information in helping us to compile this guide.

CONTENTS

Ready For Takeoff?

So you're in Atlanta again? What's here, you ask. And if it is here, where is it? What about all those other airports you've had to hole up in . . . O'Hare, Philadelphia, Newark. Surely there is more to them than bewildering concourses and bossy automated trains. In fact—there is.

Some are full-blown shopping centers; others can pass for art museums. You can play golf at one, dine in regal elegance at another, get your teeth cleaned at several. You can steep in a sauna in Phoenix, get a healthy dose of culture at Seattle, or just enjoy the view high atop Boston-Logan sipping a bottle of the local brew.

The point is, they all offer different amenities, and with this guide you can make the most of your sojourn. The next time you're stuck in San Francisco because the fog snuck in the backdoor and delayed your departure for three hours, don't wonder what to do. With a confident and somewhat smug air of the seasoned traveler, casually open this book and you'll know.

QUICK REFERENCE

AIRLINE	TELEPHONE	CODE
Aer Lingus	1–800–223–6537	EI
Aerolineas Argentinas	1–800–333–0276	AR
(FL)	1–800–432–8115	
Aero Vias de Mexico	1–800–237–6639	AM
Aeroperu	1–800–255–7378	PL
Air America	1–800–247–2475	GM
(CA)	1–800–654–8880	
Air Canada	1–800–422–6232	AC
Air France	1–800–237–2747	AF
Air India	1–800–223–7776	AI
Air Jamaica	1–800–523–5585	JM
Air Midwest	1–800–272–6433	ZV
Air New Zealand	1–800–262–1234	TE
Air Panama	1–800–272–6262	AP
Air Sedona	1–800–535–4448	UJ
Alaska Airlines	1–800–426–0333	AS
Alia Royal Jordanian	1–800–223–0470	RJ
Alitalia	1–800–223–5730	AZ
Allegheny Commuter	1–800–428–4253	US
All Nippon Air	1–800–235–9262	AN
Aloha Airlines	1–800–227–4900	AQ
America West	1–800–247–5692	HP
American Airlines	1–800–433–7300	AA
Australian Airlines	1–800–922–5122	AU
Austrian Airlines	1–800–843–0002	AS
Avensa	1–800–872–3533	VE
Avianca	1–800–284–2622	AV
BWIA International	1–800–327–7401	BW
Braniff	1–800–272–6433	BN
British Airways	1–800–247–9297	BA
Canadian Airline International	1–800–426–7000	CP
Cathay Pacific	1–800–233–2742	CX
China Air	1–800–227–5118	CI
Continental	1–800–525–0280	CO

Airline	Phone	Code
Czechoslovak Airlines	1–800–223–2365	OK
Delta	1–800–221–1212	DL
Delta Connection	1–800–345–3400	
(ASA, Comair, Business Express, Skywest)		
Eastern	1–800–327–8376	EA
(UT)	1–800–367–2139	
Ecuatoriana	1–800–328–2367	EU
(FL)	1–800–626–0363	EI
El Al Israel	1–800–223–6700	LY
Finnair	1–800–223–5700	AY
Garuda Indonesian	1–800–248–2829	GA
Guyana Air	1–800–242–4210	GY
Havasu Airlines	1–800–528–8047	HW
(AZ)	1–800–824–6614	
Hawaiian Airlines	1–800–367–5320	HA
Horizon Air	1–800–547–9308	AS
Iberia	1–800–772–4642	IB
Icelandair	1–800–221–6640	FI
Japan Air	1–800–525–3663	JL
KLM	1–800–777–5553	KL
LACSA	1–800–225–2272	LR
Lan Chile Airlines	1–800–735–5526	LA
Las Vegas Airlines	1–800–634–6851	PQ
LOT Polish Airlines	1–800–223–0593	LO
Lufthansa	1–800–645–3880	LH
MGM Grand Air	1–800–422–1101	MG
Malev Hungarian	1–800–223–6884	MA
Mexicana	1–800–531–7921	MX
Midway Airlines	1–800–621–5700	ML
Midwest Express	1–800–452–2022	YX
Northwest	1–800–225–2525	NW
Olympic	1–800–223–1226	OA
Pakistan	1–800–221–2552	PK
Pan Am	1–800–221–1111	PA
Philippine Airlines	1–800–435–9725	PR
Piedmont Airlines	1–800–251–5720	PI
Qantas Airways	1–800–227–4500	QA
(CA)	1–800–622–0850	
Royal Air Maroc	1–800–344–6726	AT
Sabena (NY)	1–800–632–8050	SN
(East Coast)	1–800–645–3700	
(South, Midwest)	1–800–645–3790	
(West)	1–800–645–1382	
Saudia	1–800–472–8342	SV
Scandinavian Air	1–800–221–2350	SK
Singapore Airlines	1–800–742–3333	SQ

Skywest	1–800–453–9417	OO
(UT)	1–800–662–4237	
Sunworld	1–800–722–4111	JK
Swissair	1–800–221–4750	SR
TACA	1–800–535–8780	TA
TWA	1–800–892–4141	TW
(International)		
(Domestic)	1–800–221–2000	
TAP Air Portugal	1–800–221–7370	TP
Thai Airways	1–800–426–5204	TG
USAir	1–800–428–4322	US
United	1–800–241–6522	UA
Varig Brazilian	1–800–468–2744	RG
(FL)	1–800–432–4420	
Viasa Venezuelan	1–800–327–5454	VA
(FL)	1–800–432–3648	
Virgin Atlantic Air	1–800–522–3084	ZP
Wardair Canada	1–800–237–0314	WD
(FL)	1–800–282–4571	
Yugoslav Air	1–800–752–6528	JU

CAR RENTAL AGENCIES

Agency Rent A Car	1–800–321–1972
(OH)	1–800–362–1794
Airways	1–800–323–8515
(IL)	1–800–671–7070
Alamo	1–800–327–9633
American Int'l	1–800–527–0202
Avis	1–800–331–1212
Budget	1–800–527–0700
(TX)	1–800–442–0700
Dollar	1–800–421–6868
Enterprise	1–800–325–8007
Exchange	1–800–327–2836
General	1–800–327–7607
Hertz	1–800–654–3131
(AK, HI)	1–800–654–8200
(OK)	1–800–522–3711
National	1–800–227–7368
Payless	1–800–237–2804
Rent-Rite	1–800–243–7483
Sears	1–800–527–0770
(TX)	1–800–442–0770
Snappy	1–800–669–4800
(OH)	1–800–321–0736
Thrifty	1–800–367–2277
USA	1–800–872–2277

International Symbols

Bank (Currency Exchange)		Information		
Bar/Lounge		Lockers		
Car Rental		Lost And Found		
Chapel		Mail		
Customs		Restaurant		
Duty-Free Shop		Rest Rooms		
Elevator/Escalator		Snack Bar		
First Aid		Shops (Gifts/News)		
Ground Transportation		Ticketing		
Immigration		Traveler's Aid		

Airports

ATLANTA

HARTSFIELD–ATLANTA INTERNATIONAL AIRPORT

Old Joke, New Twist
Traveler's Epitaph: "I know not my
final destination, only that I will
have to change planes in Atlanta."

The busiest and biggest connecting hub in the world, Atlanta International Airport is a curious mixture of Northern efficiency and Southern charm.

Almost 48 million people in 1987 trod the concourses of ATL, giving it the distinction of being No. 2 in passenger movement (Chicago's O'Hare is No. 1) in the world. Between simulated human voices and computer operated trains, passengers are whisked from concourse to concourse with robotic efficiency. Even the Swiss would be envious.

The airport was named after William B. Hartsfield who was mayor of Atlanta from 1937 to 1961.

ATL is the second largest "city" in Georgia, with over 150,000 passengers and employees daily traversing its six square miles. Georgia's major employment center, ATL generates $6 billion annually.

ATL has one of the largest art collections in an airport, funded by grants from the Atlanta City Council, the National Endowment for the Arts, the FAA, and the airlines. The art chosen is avant-garde. Neons, banners, acrylics and metal works abound. You would have to be comatose not to notice.

Boiled peanuts—probably no other airport but ATL sells this hot item. Warning: they're habit-forming, messy and may cause chapped lips.

QUICK CONTACTS
Medical. . . . 911
Police . . . 911

Lost & Found. . . . 530–2100
Information. . . . 530–6600
Paging. . . . Airlines

THE BASICS

Name: William B. Hartsfield Atlanta International
Airport
Airport Code: ATL
Location: 9 miles south of Atlanta
Mailing Address: Hartsfield International Airport
Atlanta, GA 30320
Telephone: (404) 530–6600
Time: Eastern
Daily Passenger (Rank): 137,500 (2)
Supervising Body: Atlanta City Council
Department of Aviation

AIRLINE	TELEPHONE	CONCOURSE
Air Jamaica	1–800–523–5585	INT
American	521–2655	D
ASA	996–4872	D
BahamasAir	321–0331	D
Braniff	530–4316	D
British Airways	763–0740	INT
British Caledonian	577–3510	INT
Cayman Airways	366–8519	INT
Continental	584–6621	C,D,INT
Delta	765–5000	A,B,C,D,INT
Eastern	435–1111	B,C,INT
Eastern Atlantic	435–1111	C
Eastern Metro	762–2724/2746	C
Japan Air Lines	1–800–424–9235	INT
KLM	1–800–556–7777	INT
Lufthansa	530–3780	INT
Midway	530–4070	D

AIRLINE	TELEPHONE	CONCOURSE
Midwest Express	530–2466	D
Northwest	530–2434	D
Pan Am	1–800–221–1111	D
Piedmont	681–3100	D
Sabena	1–800–654–3790	INT
Swissair	956–9704	INT
TWA	522–5738	D
United	394–2234	D
USAir	530–3516	D

FINDING YOUR WAY AROUND

ATL is composed of two terminals, North and South, which are joined by connecting "bridges" lined with concessions and car rental agencies. Baggage claim and storage are also in this area. The terminals feed four domestic concourses; A is the closest. An underground transit mall connects concourses and terminals by means of a subway that can move approximately 400 passengers every two minutes. Moving sidewalks run parallel to the trains and a walkway. Directories are located at each concourse on either side of the escalators. Monitors with airline information are plentiful.

The International Concourse adjoins the North Terminal and is self-contained. To assist foreign travelers, the lower level of the International Concourse contains an information counter, staffed by multilingual personnel, and a currency exchange.

INFORMATION FOR THE HANDICAPPED

ATL conforms to Architectural and Transportation Barriers Compliance standards. If you require special assistance, notify the airline you are traveling with ahead of time. TDD units are located near the escalators at all concourses and at the Travelers Aid in the North Terminal.

GROUND TRANSPORTATION

Ground transportation including hotel shuttles is located at the western end of the terminal complex.

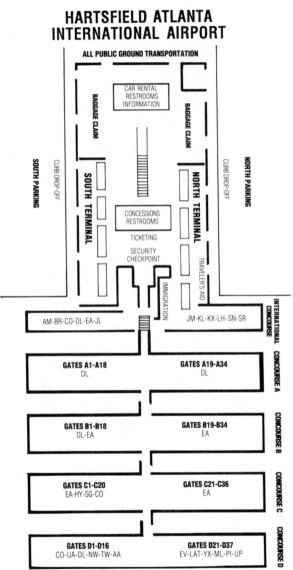

HARTSFIELD ATLANTA
INTERNATIONAL AIRPORT

ATLANTA METRO

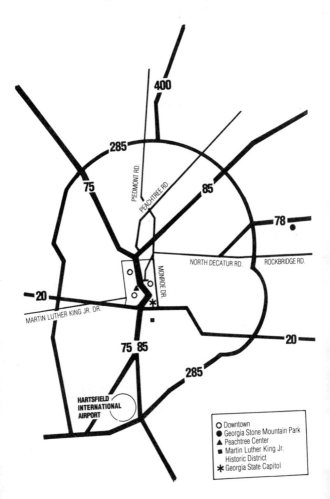

MARTA, Atlanta's rapid transit system is located at the western end of the South Terminal, is the cheapest way to get downtown.

Buses/Rapid Transit (MARTA)

Nonstop shuttle bus to downtown area costs $7/one way, $12/round-trip. It runs every 15 minutes, 5:30 a.m.–12:30 a.m.

A MARTA station is located on the lower level at the western end of the Terminal complex. MARTA's train system operates 7 days a week, 5 a.m. to approximately 2 a.m. The trains run from 6 to 15 minutes apart. The fare: $.85 for any destination. Airport to downtown: approximately 20 minutes/one way.

Car Rentals

Agencies are located on the western connecting bridge in the Terminal complex.

Alamo	768–8855	Dollar	530–3100
Avis	530–2700	Hertz	530–2900
Budget	530–3000	National	530–2800

Hotel Shuttles

Free shuttles to hotels run about every 15 minutes from the ground transport area. Courtesy phones are located on the western connecting bridge and in the shuttle lot.

Taxis/Limos

Taxis: Airport to downtown: $13.50/person; 2 people/ $7 each; 3 or more/$5 each. Airport bullpen telephone: 530–6698

Limos: $15—$25, depending on destination.
A-1 Limousine Service Inc.: 299–2388
Executive Limousine: 458–2200

Parking

Short term parking: $1/hr.; $12/day
Long term parking: $6/day
West Autopark: $5/24 hrs., $2 for each additional 12 hr. period.
Airport Park-Ride: $4/24 hrs., $2 for each additional 12

hr. period. Free shuttle to terminal.
Econo-Park: $3/day.
For additional information, call 530–6725.

TRAVELERS SERVICES

The services and facilities at ATL are a cut above
average. Shops sell everything from T-shirts to Gucci
bags, and food ranges from sausage dogs to seafood
buffets.

Airline Clubs

American's Admiral	D-27
Continental's President's Club	B-2, C-26
Delta's Crown Room	A-18
Eastern's Ionosphere	B-24, C-25
Piedmont's Presidential Suite	D-27
TWA's World Club	D-27

Baggage Storage

Storage Room: North Terminal, eastern end, 1–3 bags/
$5 a day. Lockers are located in all concourses and in
the Terminal complex. $1/24 hrs.

Banks

First Atlanta National Bank
North Terminal, eastern end. Full service bank.
Open M–F, 9 a.m. to 4 p.m. Call: 768–2856
DEK International Currency Exchange
M–F, 9 a.m. to 8:30 p.m., Sat. & Sun., 11:30 a.m. to
8:30 p.m. Call 761–6331
Express Cash—Eastern and Delta Baggage Claim
areas.
Automatic Teller Machines (3)
1—adjacent to First Atlanta
2—one on each connecting bridge

Business Services

Mutual of Omaha Service Center: Eastern connecting
bridge. Travel insurance, notary, secretarial services,
etc. can all be found there.
6 a.m. to 9 p.m. daily. 761–0106

Cocktail Lounges

All concourses, Terminal complex
ATL's Lounges are famous for their Bloody Marys
($3.25). They're the best—try them.

Gift Shops/Newsstands

All concourses, Terminal complex.
Some special features: the Grove, a fruit and nut shop
(Terminal, Concourse B), and a Country Store, selling
hams, jams and selected "down home" items
(Terminal, Concourse B).

Information/Assistance

Georgia Welcome Station: Escalator exit, Terminal
complex
Traveler's Aid: North Terminal
Crisis counseling, limited financial assistance, social
agency referral. M–F, 10 a.m. to 6 a.m. Call 766–4511

Military Services

USO: North Terminal. Sun.—Th., 10 a.m. to
8 p.m.; F, 10 a.m. to 9 p.m. Sat., 10 a.m. to 6 p.m.
Call 761–8061

Miscellaneous

Game Room/video arcade: Terminal complex.
Chapel (Interfaith): Terminal complex.
Shoeshine: Terminal complex.
Photo Machines: Terminal complex, Concourse B, D.
Barbershop: Terminal complex, Concourse C.
Florist: Concourse A, C.

Post

Stamp vending machines, mail drops: All concourses,
Terminal complex.

Restaurants/Snack Bars

Food is the standard fare and over-priced only
slightly. A cheeseburger and soda will run $4.50,
coffee is $.75, and beer is $2.25. Concourses A, B, and
C have cafeteria-style snack bars where you can dine
passably for under $7. Fresh shrimp and oysters on
the half-shell are offered at the restaurant near A-28.
Gourmet ice cream shops (double-scoop, $2.30) are

located on all concourses except D, but D boasts the only frozen yogurt stand.

Passport II is a full-service restaurant located on the Eastern bridge, Terminal complex. Open 7 days, 7 a.m. to 9:30 p.m.

Snack shops: All concourses, Terminal complex.

TIME TO KILL

1 hour. . . . Not much time but there is a video arcade area. Or you could admire the art. ATL has an impressive display of contemporary art. Let your mind wander and forget the maddening crowds and the delays.

2 hours. . . . Spend 85 cents and be adventurous. Ride 26 miles on the MARTA and pass through Atlanta faster than Sherman. You'll get a quick read of both the good and the bad in this sprawling and vibrant city.

3 hours. . . . The Carter Presidential Center. Peruse the 27 million pages of documents and the 1.5 million photographs. Open M–Sat., 9 a.m. to 5 p.m., Sun., noon to 5 p.m. Admission is $2.50 for Adults, $1.50 for Senior citizens, free to children under 16. Take MARTA to Five Points Station, then Bus #16 to Linwood. Call 331–3942.

4 hours. . . . Cyclorama. Atlantans are unanimous: this is the one attraction that's a must-see if you have the time. An immense painting in the round enhanced by 3-D figures, this unique attraction was completed in 1885 and depicts the 1864 Battle of Atlanta. Open 7 days, 9:20 a.m. to 4:30 p.m. Take MARTA to Five Points, Bus #31 to Grant Park. Admission is $3. It is worth it. Call 658–7625

And while you are there—the Atlanta Zoo is conveniently located next door to Cyclorama. Admission is $5.25 for adults, $2.25 for children. Open to 5:00 p.m. daily. Call 622-ROAR

For additional information call the Atlanta Convention and Visitors Bureau (404) 521–6600 or (404) 767–3231 (Airport).

BOSTON

BOSTON–LOGAN
INTERNATIONAL AIRPORT

This is a convenient, easy-to-get-around, and downright hospitable airport. Modern Pilgrims will find all the amenities and little fluff. It's a nice place to kill a couple of hours and you probably will. The weather gets nasty in New England occasionally and getting boxed in is not uncommon.

Logan was named for Lieutenant General Edward L. Logan, a WW I military figure and prominent Massachusetts statesman.

Logan/South Harborside (the air cargo/aviation service annex) is a $200 million complex built on "Bird Island Flats"—90 acres snatched from Boston Harbor.

Logan people prefer to call lousy weather "adverse." In any case they are well-prepared to fight it with a fleet of blowers, plows, pushers, and scrapers. Twenty-one snow melters can melt 80 tons of snow per hour. That's enough water to fill 200 swimming pools in Framingham.

The BOS Control Tower is the tallest at any airport, standing 300 feet.

This is probably the only airport in the U.S. where a passenger could get "bumped" because a ship is in the harbor. FAA rules require a take-off weight lighter by 10,000 lbs. if a vessel is moving or anchored off the end of the runways. It hasn't happened yet, but if it did something would have to go: fuel, baggage, or possibly you.

QUICK CONTACTS

Medical Services. . . . 567–2020
Police. . . . 567–2233
Lost & Found. . . . 561–1806
Information . . . 561–1800
Paging . . . Airlines

THE BASICS

Name: Boston–Logan International Airport
Airport Code: BOS
Location: East Boston Harbor, Suffolk County,
          Massachusetts
Mailing Address: Logan International Airport
                 East Boston, MA 02128
Telephone: (617) 561–1800
Time: Eastern
Daily Passengers (Rank): 59,900 (13)

Supervising Body: Massachusetts Port Authority
                  (MassPort)

AIRLINES	TELEPHONES	TERMINAL
Aer Lingus	1–800–223–6537	E
Air Atlantic	1–800–565–1890	E
Air Canada	1–800–442–6232	E
Air France	1–800–237–2747	E
Air Nova	1–800–422–6232	E
Alitalia	1–800–223–5730	E
American	542–6700	B
American Eagle	1–800–433–7300	B
Braniff	1–800–272–6433	B
British Airways	1–800–247–9297	E
Butler Aviation	567–8010	D
Catskill	1–800–833–0196	B
Continental	1–800–525–0280	B
Continental Shuttle	1–800–525–0280	A
Delta	567–4100	C

AIRLINES	TELEPHONE	TERMINAL
Delta Connection	567–4100	C
Eastern	262–3700	A
Eastern/Bar Harbor	262–3700	A
Eastern/ Precision	1–800–451–4221	A
El Al Israel	1–800–223–6700	E
First Air	1–800–422–6232	E
Henson/ Piedmont Reg.	523–1100	B
HubExpress	1–800–452–2022	B
Icelandia	1–800–223–5500	E
Long Island Air	516–752–8300	B
Lufthansa	1–800–645–3880	E
Midway	1–800–621–5700	C
Midwest Express	1–800–452–2022	B
Northwest	267–4885	E
PanAm Express	1–800–223–1115	B
PanAm Shuttle	1–800–223–5160	B
Piedmont	523–1100	B
Provincetown-Boston	567–6090	A
Sabena	1–800–645–3700	B
Sabena (International)	1–800–645–3700	E
Swissair	1–800–221–4750	E
TAP	1–800–221–7370	E
TWA	367–2800	C
TWA (International)	367–2800	E
USAir	482–3160	B
United	482–7900	C
Valley Air	1–800–322–1008	A
Van Dusen	569–5260	D

FINDING YOUR WAY AROUND

There is nothing complicated about BOS. Five
terminals, all designated by alphabetical letters and
color-coded, form a horseshoe around the central
parking garage. Terminal E is the International facility

LOGAN
INTERNATIONAL AIRPORT

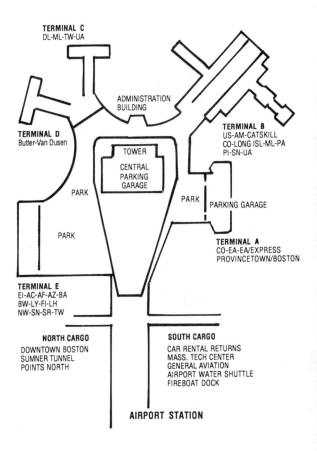

BOSTON METRO AREA

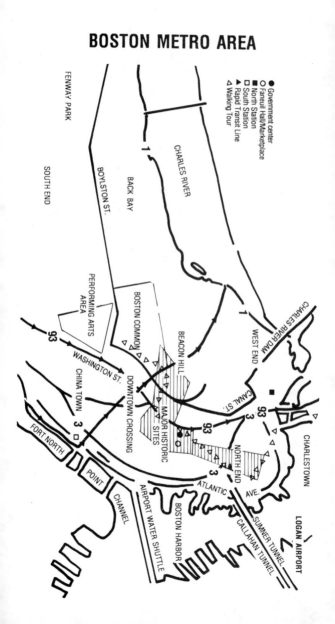

and houses U.S. Customs/Immigration. Free shuttle
buses run every eight minutes between the terminals.

FACILITIES FOR THE HANDICAPPED

BOS meets standards as promulgated by the
Architectural and Transportation Barriers Compliance
Board. Special shuttles for the handicapped for inter-
terminal connections are available. TDD phones are
located at the information booths in Terminals A, C,
and E.

GROUND TRANSPORTATION

Logan offers one of the most extensive ground
transport systems serving any airport. There are
subways, shuttles, taxis, limos, public buses,
handicapped vans, scheduled buses serving all of
New England and even a water taxi. Pick up a
transportation brochure at any of the information
desks in the terminals, or call 1–800–23-LOGAN.
If you're traveling light to downtown, take the
subway; if the weather is decent and this is your one
trip to Boston, take the water shuttle.

Buses/Rapid Transit

Buses #22 and #33 service between terminals and to
T-Subway Airport Station. Bus #11 services terminals
only. Hours: 5:30 a.m. to 1 a.m., daily. Buses leave
every 10 minutes. Free.
Express buses run to Quincy Adams Station and
Framingham. Every 30 minutes M–F; every 60
minutes S–Sun. Fare is $5/$7 respectively, children
under 12 ride free.
Handicapped vans are free between terminals. Use
Van Phone in baggage claims areas, or call 561–1769.
THEM, Inc. (494–0200) and The Ride (722–5123) are
specially equipped delivery vehicles for points
throughout the area.
The T Blue Line runs from Airport Station to
downtown Boston daily, 5:25 a.m. to 1 a.m., every 8
to 12 minutes. Fare is 60 cents.

Car Rentals

Agency counters are located in the baggage claims area of each terminal.

Alamo	561–4100	Dollar	569–5300
American	569–3550	Hertz	569–7272
Avis	424–0800	National	569–6700
Budget	569–4000	USA	561–0503

Hotel Shuttles

Courtesy phone banks are located in the baggage claim area of each terminal.

Taxis/Limos

All terminals. Fare is $10/one-way to downtown area, flat rates for other points.

Water Shuttle

It's a seven-minute ride from the Logan Boat Dock to Rowes Wharf. M–F, 6 a.m. to 8 p.m.; S–Sun, noon to 8 p.m. Fare is $6/adults, $3/under 12.

Parking

All lots, including the central garage, are $2/hr., $10 daily maximum. Avoid the "D" lot unless you're absolutely sure you're a short-termer—there is no maximum.

TRAVELERS SERVICES

Massport keeps an eye on prices so the unwary don't get gouged. Terminal C, extensively renovated in the last five years, is the focal point for amenities and worth a visit with its kinetic sculptures and shifting ceiling sails.

Airline Clubs

American's Admiral	Terminal B
Delta's Crown	Terminal C
Eastern's Ionosphere	Terminal A
Northwest's World Club	Terminal E
TWA's Ambassador	Terminal C
United's Red Carpet	Terminal C
British Air, Lufthansa, SwissAir	Terminal E.

Baggage Storage

Coin lockers only; all terminals, concourses. $.75/ 24hrs.

Banks

Bay Bank Currency Exchange: Daily/11:30 a.m. to 9:30 p.m., Terminal E. Bay Bank also operates a full service facility on Airport Entry Road, across from Terminal E. Hours: M–W, 9 a.m., to 4 p.m., Th–Sat. 9 a.m. to 6 p.m.
Auto Teller Machines (ATMs): all terminals.
American Express Cash units: Terminal A, near Eastern Counter Term. B, near American counter.

Business Services

There are none as of this writing. However, BOS folks tell us there may be a counter by June.

Cocktail Lounges

You won't find any Happy Hours or 2-for-1 specials here—state law forbids such come-ons. A draft beer runs $2.25; Sam Adams beer, a local favorite brewed and bottled in Boston, is $3.30. Two popular spots are the Satellite in Terminal C, and the Tower in the (you guessed it) Observation Tower. All lounges close at 1 a.m.

Gift Shops/Newsstands

Shops and newsstands provide the basic travelers needs with some notable exceptions. Hello Boston and Legal Seafood are two vendors who sell lobsters (and live ones at that) to go. Prices start at $7.95/lb., plus $3.50 for the packaging. They'll keep for 48 hours. Both vendors are open daily. Benjamin Books in Terminal C is open daily, 7 a.m. to 10 p.m.

Hotel

The on-site Logan Hilton has 542 rooms. A single during the week starts at $125; on weekends, at $99. Call 569–9300.

Information/Assistance

Terminal A: daily, 7:30 a.m. to 11:30 p.m.
Terminal C: daily, 7:30 a.m. to 11 p.m.
Terminal E: summer only, noon to 8 p.m.

Travelers Aid:

Terminal A, daily/9 a.m. to midnight
Terminal E, daily/noon to 7 a.m. Call 542-7286.

Military Services

USO located in Terminal D.
Hours M-F, 9 to 8 p.m.
Sat, 11 a.m. to 7 p.m.
Sun, 11 a.m. to 6 p.m.

Miscellaneous

Barbershops: Located in all terminals. M–F,
7:30 a.m. to 6 p.m. Sat, 9 a.m. to 6 p.m.
Shoeshine: Terminal C. Daily, 6:30 a.m. to
8 p.m.
Chapel: Non-denominational, Terminal C. The "Our
Lady of the Airways" chapel held its first services in
1952.
Dental Clinic: Terminal B, M–Th, 8:30 a.m. to
5 p.m.
Medical: MGH-Logan Health Assoc., Terminal D.
M–F, 8:30 a.m. to 5 p.m. Call 726-3570.
Nursery Facilities: Terminal C. Also "Kidport," a
mini-playground with a view of the runways.

Post

Mail drops and stamp vending machines in all
terminals.

Restaurants/Snack Bars

BOS has 16 snack bars, coffee shops, and restaurants,
but you can't get Boston baked beans at any one of
them. A snack bar burger is $1.75, a bowl of chowder,
$2.25. Ogden's in Terminal C is a sitdown restaurant
that is open daily to 10 p.m. A lobster dinner is $18;
but if you lean toward beef the New York sirloin is
$10.50. And if you're really adventurous, try the
Arigato Sushi Bar in Terminal E.

TIME TO KILL

1 hour. . . . Weather permitting, the Tower (16th floor) between Terminals B and C offers a spectacular view of the Boston skyline from its observation deck. If the weather does not permit, try the 17th floor cocktail lounge for views over glass. It's open from 9 a.m. to 11 p.m.

2 hours. . . . Need your teeth cleaned? $35. Logan is one of the very few airports in the world that has a dental clinic. It's in Terminal B. Open M–Th, 8:30 a.m. to 5 p.m. You'll need an appointment. Call (617) 569–0006.

3 hours. . . . The T will put you in downtown in 15 minutes for 60 cents. A short walk from the Government Center station is the Quincy Market, Faneuil Hall complex, which has become a major tourist attraction. Full of shops, restaurants, and sidewalk entertainment, this area of restored 19th century market houses offers everything from folk art to fine silver to whimsical kites. The Union Oyster House has been shucking oysters since 1826. Market shops are open M–Sat., 9 a.m. to 9 p.m.; Sun., noon to 6 p.m.

4 hours . . . If you catch the time right, Old Towne Trolley offers a 90-minute tour of Boston. You'll see Bunker Hill and the USS Constitution. Trolley tours start from the New England Aquarium, the second stop after leaving BOS via the T. It runs daily until 5 p.m. during the summer months and until 3 p.m. during the winter. Price: $11 for adults, $4 for children under 12. Call 269–7010. Or try the Aquarium. Hours: M–Th, 9 a.m. to 5 p.m.; F, 9 a.m. to 9 p.m.; S–Sun, 9 a.m. to 6 p.m. Admission is $6 for adults and $3.50 for children.

What's New New England tourism information centers are located in Terminals C, E. Or for additional information call the Boston Convention and Visitors Bureau (617) 536–4100.

CHARLOTTE

CHARLOTTE/DOUGLAS INTERNATIONAL AIRPORT

This airport zoomed from a modest regional facility to major import in the aftermath of deregulation. Passenger volume in 1980 was 3.1 million; by the end of 1987, Charlotte was handling a staggering 13 million—a 425 percent increase. Such phenomenal growth rendered previous plans obsolete and Charlotte has embarked on yet another master plan that assumes a 187 percent growth rate in the next 16 years. The airport is a $1 billion a year force in the Charlotte-Mecklenburg economy and has been a key factor in attracting corporate relocations.

So who was Douglas? Charlotte's first passenger terminal, built in the 1940's, was named for Mayor Ben E. Douglas who was instrumental in promoting the city as an aviation stop.

That's Queen Charlotte reigning over the reflecting pool. Executed by sculptor Raymond Kaskey, the $250,000 15-foot, bronze statue was largely financed by the Queens Table, a group of Charlotteans of civic bent.

QUICK CONTACTS

Medical . . . 359–4012
Police . . . 359–4010
Lost & Found . . . 359–4012
Information . . . 359–4013
Paging . . . 359–4013

THE BASICS

Name: Charlotte/Douglas International Airport
Airport Code: CLT
Telephone: (704) 359–4000
Location: 6 miles west of Charlotte, NC
Mailing Address: 6501 Old Dowd Road
                 Charlotte, NC 28214

Time: Eastern
Daily Passengers (Rank): 35, 558 (34)
Supervising Body: City of Charlotte

AIRLINE	TELEPHONE	LOCATION
American	333–0130	A
Delta	372–3000	A
Eastern	366–6131	B
Pan Am	359–0113	A
Piedmont	376–0235	B,C
TWA	359–4632	A
United	359–4406	A
USAir	359–4550	A

FINDING YOUR WAY AROUND

Terminal layout is typical: a main two-level complex
with four concourses radiating outward. Since this is
a major hub for the USAir/Piedmont group, most
passenger traffic is concentrated in B and C
concourses. CLT is and will be for sometime under
construction.

INFORMATION FOR THE HANDICAPPED

CLT provides facilities for handicapped and elderly
travelers in accordance with standards of the
Architectural and Transportation Barriers Compliance
Board. All travelers with special needs are advised to
notify their air carriers prior to departure. A TDD unit
is located at the Pre-Pay counter on the lower level.

GROUND TRANSPORTATION

All ground transportation departs from the lower
level of the main terminal. CLT stations air host/

hostesses in front of the terminal to guide travelers and answer questions.

Buses

Public buses run every hour in the mornings and evenings only. The fare to downtown is $.70.

Hotel Shuttles

Courtesy phones are located in both wings of the lower level of the terminal.

Rental Cars

Rental car counters are located on the lower level. On-site agencies are:

Alamo	392–8020	Dollar	359–4700
Avis	359–4580	Hertz	359–0114
Budget	359–5000	National	359–4652

Taxis

For information regarding taxis, call Yellow Cab, 332–6161. The fare to downtown is $11 for one person, $2 each for extra passengers.

Parking

CLT has garage parking for 2,000 vehicles and 7,000 open lot spaces. Short term rates are: $.75/half hr., $6 daily max. Long term rates are: $.50/hr., $4 daily max. Remote parking lot rates are $2/day. Free shuttles run from the remote lot to the terminal.

Travelers Services

Most travelers amenities are located on the upper level of the main terminal, although lounges and snack bars line the concourses.

Airline Clubs

Piedmont has Presidential Suites located on Concourses B and C.

Baggage Storage

Coin lockers only. Rates are $.50/24 hrs.

Banks

1st Citizens Bank is on the upper level of the terminal. Hours are: M–Th, 9 a.m. to 5 p.m.; F, 9 a.m. to 6 p.m.

Business Services

At present there are no business services at CLT.

Cocktail Lounges

The Blue Crab lounge/raw bar is located on Concourse B. Hours are daily, 8 a.m. to 9:30 p.m. There are lounges on each concourse and one in the main terminal.

Gift Shops/Newsstands

The Country Store on the upper level specializes in Carolina arts and crafts. "Fantasies" is a women's boutique specializing in . . . well, uh . . . fantasies.

Information/Assistance

An information booth is located on the upper level of the main terminal. Open around-the-clock. Call 359–4013.

Military Services

There are no military services at CLT.

Miscellaneous

Barbershop/shoeshine: East end of the lower level in the main terminal.
Nursery changing rooms: Adjacent to the restrooms in the ground floor area.
Video game room: It's on the upper level. Open 24 hours.

Restaurants/Snack Bars

Pizza Strada is in the main terminal. The hours are daily from 7 a.m. to 9 p.m. There are seven stand-up snackbars throughout the complex.

Post

Mail drops are located throughout the complex.

Time to Kill

For a short layover, bring a book. You can feed the video machines in the game room, or just people watch. CLT is a facility trying to catch up to its growth. If you have more time . . .

3 hours . . . The Discovery Place in downtown Charlotte is a "hands-on" museum, complete with a planetarium and a solarium. Open M-Sat, 9 a.m. to 6 p.m.; Sun, 1 p.m. to 6 p.m. Admission is $4.

4 hours . . . The Charlotte Coliseum, besides being home to the Hornets of the NBA, also schedules concerts and shows. For box office information call 376–6864.

For additional information, call the Charlotte Convention and Visitors Bureau, 371–8700, or 1–800–231–4636.

CHICAGO

CHICAGO–O'HARE INTERNATIONAL AIRPORT

Jet travel made O'Hare. In 1959, O'Hare wasn't even the largest airport serving Chicago; that distinction belonged to Midway. But O'Hare had one tangible Midway did not—space. Jets needed space and O'Hare, out on the northwest fringe, had plenty of it. A decision was made and the rest, as they say, is history. From a small passenger volume of 2 million a year in 1960, O'Hare has outstripped all other airports. It's the largest mover of people in the world; over 57 million travelers march its concourses each year. And there's no let up in sight as that number is forecast to hit 82 million by 1995.

O'Hare is undergoing a gradual facelift. The present $1.6 billion renovation includes the addition of varied and unusual shops, improved and generally good eating concessions, and modernistic new construction.

O'Hare is named for Edward H. "Butch" O'Hare, a WW II pilot and Congressional Medal of Honor winner who was killed in combat in 1943.

The code "ORD" is a holdover from Orchard Place, the site of a WW II military facility. Average per acre purchase price—$700.

President John F. Kennedy, guest of honor at the O'Hare dedication in 1963, said: "This is an extraordinary airport . . . and it could be classed as one of the wonders of the world." Consider the following superlatives:

A plane lands or takes off from ORD every 41 seconds—a total of 789,000 flight operations each year.

On-premises airline kitchens prepare over 45,000 in-flight meals a day.

Underneath its runway-terminal complex, ORD has 90 miles of fuel lines, sewers, and water pipes.

Over 200,000 passengers will fly in or out of ORD on its two busiest days—the Wednesday before Thanksgiving and the Sunday after.

QUICK CONTACTS

Medical . . . 686–2288 (First Aid)
            686–2244 (Trauma)
Police . . . 686–2230
Lost & Found . . . 686–2201
Information . . . 686–2200
Paging . . . 686–2200

THE BASICS

Name: Chicago O'Hare International Airport
Airport Code: ORD
Location: 17 miles northwest of Chicago
Mailing Address: PO Box 66142
            Chicago, Ill 60666
Telephone: (312) 686–2200
Time: Central
Daily Passengers (Rank): 154,194 (1)
Supervising Body: City of Chicago
            Department of Aviation

AIRLINE	TELEPHONE	TERMINAL
Air Canada	1–800–422–6232	3
Air France	1–800–237–2747	3
ALIA	236–1702	4
Alitalia	427–4720	4
American	372–8000	3
American Eagle	372–8000	3
American Trans Air	686–6522	4

AIRLINE	TELEPHONE	TERMINAL
Braniff	1–800–272–6433	2
British	786–1340	4
Cayman	1–800–422–9626	4
Comair	1–800–354–9822	3
Condor	1–800–645–3880	3
Continental	686–6500	2
Continental Express	1–800–652–7488	3
Delta	346–5300	3
Eastern	467–2900	2
Ecuatoriana	1–800–328–2367	4
El Al Israel	1–800–223–6700	4
Great Lakes	1–800–554–5111	2
Iberia	1–800–223–5000	4
Icelandair	1–800–223–5500	4
Japan	565–7000	3
Jat Yugoslav	782–1322	4
KLM	861–9300	4
LOT Polish	236–3388	4
Lufthansa	1–800–421–7574	3
Mexicana	1–800–531–7923	3
NACA	686–7668	4
Northwest	346–4900	2
PanAm	332–4900	4
Piedmont	263–3656	2
SAS	1–800–221–2350	4
Sabena	1–800–645–3790	4
SwissAir	641–8830	3
TWA	558–7000	3
United	569–3000	1,2
USAir	726–1201	3

FINDING YOUR WAY AROUND

Walk and walk and walk. Unlike the situation in
newer airports, ORD travelers must walk; there are no
underground trains or courtesy shuttles connecting
the four terminals. Three terminals with radiating
concourses form a horseshoe around Terminal 4 (the
International facility), the hotel and the parking
garage. Pedestrian tunnels from the lower levels of
each lead to the parking garage and CTA Station.
Security checkpoints are at the entranceways of all
concourses. The upper levels of terminals house
airline ticketing services and travelers amenities.

CHICAGO O'HARE
INTERNATIONAL AIRPORT

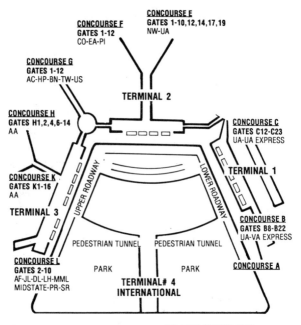

CONCOURSE E
GATES 1-10,12,14,17,19
NW-UA

CONCOURSE F
GATES 1-12
CO-EA-PI

CONCOURSE G
GATES 1-12
AC-HP-BN-TW-US

TERMINAL 2

CONCOURSE H
GATES H1,2,4,6-14
AA

CONCOURSE C
GATES C12-C23
UA-UA EXPRESS

CONCOURSE K
GATES K1-16
AA

TERMINAL 1

TERMINAL 3

UPPER ROADWAY

LOWER ROADWAY

CONCOURSE B
GATES B8-B22
UA-VA EXPRESS

PEDESTRIAN TUNNEL   PEDESTRIAN TUNNEL

CONCOURSE L
GATES 2-10
AF-JL-DL-LH-MML
MIDSTATE-PR-SR

PARK   PARK

CONCOURSE A

TERMINAL# 4
INTERNATIONAL

CTA RAPID TRANSIT AREA

LOWER LEVEL
BAGGAGE CLAIM
CAR RENTAL
GROUND TRANSPORTATION

CTA RAPID TRANSIT AVAILABLE
DOWNTOWN CHICAGO TO O'HARE
LOWER LEVEL AREA/PARK AREA

CHICAGO METRO AREA

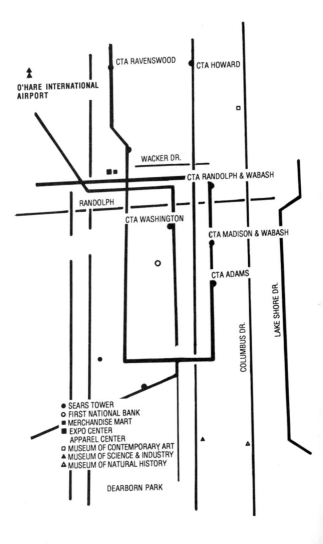

CTA RAVENSWOOD
CTA HOWARD

O'HARE INTERNATIONAL
AIRPORT

WACKER DR.

CTA RANDOLPH & WABASH

RANDOLPH

CTA WASHINGTON

CTA MADISON & WABASH

CTA ADAMS

COLUMBUS DR.

LAKE SHORE DR.

● SEARS TOWER
○ FIRST NATIONAL BANK
■ MERCHANDISE MART
■ EXPO CENTER
  APPAREL CENTER
□ MUSEUM OF CONTEMPORARY ART
▲ MUSEUM OF SCIENCE & INDUSTRY
△ MUSEUM OF NATURAL HISTORY

DEARBORN PARK

Lower levels are for baggage claim and ground transport.

INFORMATION FOR THE HANDICAPPED

ORD provides facilities for handicapped and elderly travelers in accordance with the Architectural and Transportation Barriers Compliance Board standards. TDD phones are adjacent to the Information Booths in each terminal and are accessible 24 hours a day.

GROUND TRANSPORTATION

All ground transportation is on the lower levels of the terminals and in the parking garage. Directories for all modes are on the lower levels of Terminals 2 and 3, near the baggage claim areas. The CTA elevated railway is the fastest and cheapest way to the Loop.

Buses/Rapid Transit

Information booths are on the lower levels of Terminals 2, 3, and at the curbfront of Terminal 4. The Regional Transportation Authority services the suburbs every day except Sunday. Buses depart every hour. The fare is $1. Call 836–7000.

The Continental Air Transport Co. offers scheduled service to downtown hotels and the North Shore suburbs. Vans leave every 30 minutes until 11 p.m., daily. Downtown fare is $9.75; travel time is approximately 60 minutes. Call 454–7800.

Chicago Transit Authority operates from the lower level parking garage. Take Pedestrian tunnels and watch for signs saying either "Rapid Transit" or "Trains to City." The fare is $1; time to the Loop is 35 minutes. For local information call 836–7000 or 1–800–972–7000.

Car Rentals

Agency counters are located in lower levels of all terminals.

Avis	694–5600	Hertz	686–7272
Budget	968–6661	National	694–4640
Dollar	671–5100		

Hotel Shuttles

Telephone courtesy boards are on lower levels of terminals, and in lobby of Terminal 4.

Taxis/Limos

Directories are located on lower levels, Terminals 2 & 3. Taxi curbfront booths are at each terminal. Fare to the Loop: $17.

Parking

Main Parking can accommodate 10,000 vehicles and 8,000 of the spaces are in the garage. Rates: $2 first hour, $1 each additional hour, $12 daily maximum. There are two remote lots connected to the terminals by free shuttle buses that run every 10 minutes. Rates are $1/hr., $6 /daily max.

TRAVELERS SERVICES

A metropolis of shops and services, ORD lacks only a charter to be a city. Everything from soup to nuts to lottery tickets can be purchased.

Airline Clubs

American's Admiral	Terminal 3, H-5
British Airway's Executive Lounge	Terminal 1, B-17
Continental's President's Club	Terminal 2, Mezzanine
Delta's Crown Room	L Concourse, Gate 2
Eastern's Ionosphere	Terminal 2, Mezzanine
KLM's Rembrandt Room	Terminal 4, beyond Security
Northwest's World Room	Terminal 2, E-3, Mezzanine
SAS's Scanarama	Terminal 4, beyond Security

| TWA's Ambassador | Terminal 3 |
| United's Red Carpet | Terminal 1, Concourses B & C |

(Note: Air France, Japan, Lufthansa, and Swiss Air all share facilities with Delta's Crown. Air Canada shares with TWA's Ambassador. Iberia shares with KLM.)

Baggage Storage

Coin lockers only, located in all terminals. $.75/24hr. period.

Banks

First Chicago Foreign Currency Exchange is located in Terminal 4. Hours are: S–Thurs, 10 a.m. to 8 p.m.; F–Sat, 8 a.m. to 8 p.m. Mobile currency carts also serve international flights departing from domestic gates. There is no full-service bank at ORD. Terminals 1, 2, and 3 have a liberal amount of ATMs. American Express Cash Express has three units: one located in Terminal 2 (near the United counter), and two in Terminal 3 (near the American and Delta counters).

Business Services

At the O'Hare Hilton, on the lower level, are located facilities for fax, Telex, and photocopying. Skybird meeting rooms are located between Terminals 2 and 3. The fee is $225 daily, which includes a continental breakfast. Rooms usually must be booked 2 to 4 weeks in advance. Call Carson International, (312) 686–6101.

Cocktail Lounges

Scattered throughout ORD are 27 lounges, plus the "Lightning Lounge" in the "Fast Lane" of Terminal 1. The "42nd Parallel" in the Rotunda between Terminals 2 and 3 offers beer from around the world. Or you can have a draft for $2.

Gift Shops

If you're of American Indian-Irish descent and have an unusual affliction for the Cubs, ORD has the shops for you. You can buy everything from a shillelagh to a baseball cap. Some interesting ones: Great Lakes Trading Co., Terminal 3; Irish Currents, Terminal 3;

Chicago Sports Section, Terminal 3. Cubs and White Sox caps sell for the same price ($7.95) regardless of their standings. Benjamin Books has two stores, Terminals 2 and 3, open daily, 7 a.m. to 10 p.m.

Hotel

The 25-floor O'Hare Hilton has 1,565 rooms, the most of any airport in the world. Weekday rates start at $115.

Information/Assistance

Booths are on upper levels of each Terminal and are staffed 9 a.m. to 9 p.m., daily. Between them the staff members are fluent in 18 languages.

Travelers and Immigrants Assistance is located in Terminal 2. Hours M–F, 8:30 a.m. to 9 p.m.; Sunday, noon to 9 p.m. Call 686–7562.

ORD thoughtfully provides roving, uniformed information ambassadors at key passageways. Look for the large "Airport Information" clipboards each aide carries.

Military Services

USO is in Terminal 3. Hours: Sun–F., 9 a.m. to 11 p.m.; Sat., 9 a.m. to 5 p.m. Call 686–7296.

Miscellaneous

Chapel: Basement, Terminal 2. Catholic services M–F, 11:30 a.m., Sat, 9 a.m. to 6 p.m.; Sun, 6:30 a.m., 9 a.m., 11 a.m. and 1 p.m. Protestant services Sun at 10 a.m., noon, and 2 p.m. The Airport Chaplain can be reached at 686–2636.

ORD tours are conducted M–F, at 10 a.m. and 11 a.m. Call 686–2300.

Post

Drop boxes and stamp vending machines are located in all terminals and concourses.

Restaurants/Snack Bars

ORD boasts 20 snack bars, three coffee shops, two cafeterias, one pastry shop, plus one "fine dining" facility. They are scattered throughout the complex but most are clustered in the Rotunda between Terminals 2 and 3. In the United Terminal of

Tomorrow (or Terminal 1) is the Fast Lane, a collection of fast-service restaurants (eight in all) offering everything from Mexican to lite. For fine dining, try the Seven Continents, located on the mezzanine level of the Rotunda. Recommended is the Chicken Kiev, or practically any seafood entree. Also in the Rotunda is The 42nd Parallel, which offers a raw bar. Pizza Strada in the Fast Lane is also good. All breads, rolls, cookies, etc., are baked on premises for all the restaurants. Sample price: hot dog, fries, soda—$5. Entrees at Seven Continents start at $13.

TIME TO KILL

1 hour . . . Eat or browse, or if you want to do both, go to the Fast Lane.

2 hours . . . If you make it to the Fast Lane you're in United's Terminal of Tomorrow, ORD's newest facility. A modernistic structure, enough aluminum went into its building (2 million pounds) to make 50 million beverage cans; the glass area is enough to dome both Wrigley and Commiskey Parks. In the access tunnel between B and C concourses is an awesome kinetic light sculpture and worth the walk. The last time we heard it the music was Gershwin, sort of "synthesizing in blue."

3 hours . . . Take the CTA "L" to downtown. It's only $2 and 75 minutes roundtrip. That gives you some time to wander around. The famous and at one time controversial Picasso sculpture is a block from Washington Station.

4 hours . . . For a lofty and impressive overview of the City of Big Shoulders you can't beat the $1 billion Sears Tower. Open until midnight, daily, the Tower has shops, restaurants, atriums, art, and the view from the 103rd floor is well worth the $3.75. Take the RTA to Jackson Station. Look up—you can't miss it.

The Illinois Office of Tourism staffs four offices at O'Hare, 8:30 a.m. to 5 p.m., M–F. Officers are located on the lower levels of Terminals 1, 2, and 3, and in the lobby of Terminal 4. Call 793-2094.

DALLAS

DALLAS FORT WORTH
INTERNATIONAL AIRPORT

There's nothing little about DFW. Geographically larger than the city of Newark, it produces more revenue than Baton Rouge, and has more parking spaces than Walla Walla has people. DFW has the fastest airport train, the largest airport hotel, the most runways (6) and a jumbo airport debt—all of which reflect its status as the newest (January, 1974) major airport to open in the US.

Fourth in passenger volume among the world's airports, DFW is typically Texan in ambition.

Sprawling across 10 miles and 18,000 acres, DFW is the largest air complex in the U.S., and the third largest in the world. With 26,000 parking spaces it is the largest parking lot in the country.

When excavating first began, workers uncovered the fossilized bones of a "Plesiosaur." Weighing in at 10,000 pounds, this aquatic dinosaur gives evidence that this part of Texas was once under water. (The fact that it has been buried under the runways for 70 million years has to be some kind of record for layovers.)

DFW is so huge that it has not one, but *two* 18-hole championship golf courses on-site. Both are rated in the top 50 of resort courses in the US.

And if the dinosaur and the golf courses don't set DFW apart, try these: DFW has three cemeteries. They were there before there was an airport, and they're still there. DFW also has an airport farmer/rancher. Three thousand acres are leased for wheat and sorghum, plus cattle-raising. Besides keeping arable land in production it also saves on grounds maintenance.

QUICK CONTACTS

Medical. . . . 911
Police. . . . 911
Lost & Found. . . . 574–4454
Information . . . 574–4420
Paging. . . . Airlines Only

THE BASICS

Names: Dallas/Fort Worth International Airport
Airport Code: DFW
Location: 17 miles northwest of Dallas, 17 miles
          northeast of Ft. Worth, Texas.
Mailing Address: PO Box 610042
               D/FW Airport,TX 75261
Telephone: (214) 574–4420
Time: Central
Daily Passengers (Rank): 114,728 (4)
Supervising Body: Dallas-Ft. Worth International
                  Airport Board

AIRLINE	TELEPHONE	LOCATION
Air New Zealand	1–800–262–1234	2E
American Airlines	267–1151	2W
American Eagle	267–1151	2E
Atlantic Southeast	630–3200	4E
Braniff	357–9511	2W
British Airways	1–800–231–0270	4E
Chaparral	267–1151	2E
Continental	263–0523	2E
Delta	630–3200	4E
Executive Express II	1–800–877–3932	2W
General Aviation	573–3390	2W
Lufthansa	1–800–645–3880	2E
Metro	267–1151	2E
Mexicana	1–800–531–7921	2W
Midway	1–800–621–5700	2W
Midwest Express	1–800–452–2022	2W

AIRLINE	TELEPHONE	LOCATION
Northwest Orient	988–0405	2W
Pan Am	1–800–221–1111	2W
Piedmont	647–8823	2W
Thai International	1–800–426–5204	2W
TWA	741–6741	2W
United	988–1004	2W
USAir	1–800–428–4322	2W

FINDING YOUR WAY AROUND

You won't need a compass to find your way around, despite DFW's massive size. The four terminals are self-contained and flank either side of International Parkway. Although the semi-circle configuration means a 12-minute walk from one end of a terminal to another, that same configuration allows for a short hop from boarding gate to departure level. Inter-terminal transport is via Airtrans, the automated transit system.

FACILITIES FOR THE HANDICAPPED

DFW conforms to Architectural and Transportation Barriers Compliance Board standards. TDD phones are located at Airport Assistance Booths in each terminal.

GROUND TRANSPORTATION

Ground Transportation boards with courtesy phones are located on the second level baggage claims areas of each terminal. Push "01" for general information. If traveling solo, the best mode for getting downtown is the Super Shuttle; for 2 or more people a taxi is the best way to get downtown.

Airtrans

DFW's automated transit system provides transportation between terminals, to and from long-term parking areas and to the Hyatt-Regency on-site hotel. Stations are located on lower levels of each terminal building, in the long term parking areas and at other points. For information call 574–6001.

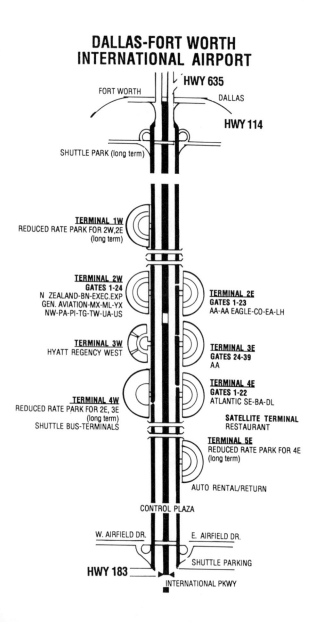

DALLAS-FORT WORTH INTERNATIONAL AIRPORT

HWY 635

FORT WORTH

DALLAS

HWY 114

SHUTTLE PARK (long term)

TERMINAL 1W
REDUCED RATE PARK FOR 2W, 2E
(long term)

TERMINAL 2W
GATES 1-24
N ZEALAND-BN-EXEC.EXP
GEN. AVIATION-MX-ML-YX
NW-PA-PI-TG-TW-UA-US

TERMINAL 2E
GATES 1-23
AA-AA EAGLE-CO-EA-LH

TERMINAL 3W
HYATT REGENCY WEST

TERMINAL 3E
GATES 24-39
AA

TERMINAL 4E
GATES 1-22
ATLANTIC SE-BA-DL

TERMINAL 4W
REDUCED RATE PARK FOR 2E, 3E
(long term)
SHUTTLE BUS-TERMINALS

SATELLITE TERMINAL
RESTAURANT

TERMINAL 5E
REDUCED RATE PARK FOR 4E
(long term)

AUTO RENTAL/RETURN

CONTROL PLAZA

W. AIRFIELD DR.

E. AIRFIELD DR.

SHUTTLE PARKING

HWY 183

INTERNATIONAL PKWY

DALLAS METRO AREA

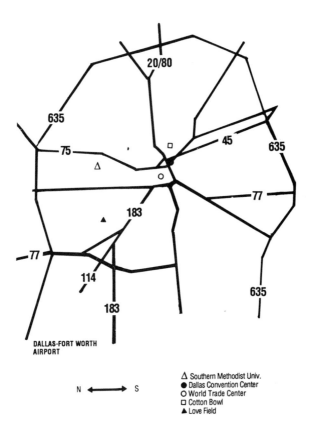

△ Southern Methodist Univ.
● Dallas Convention Center
○ World Trade Center
□ Cotton Bowl
▲ Love Field

Buses

A variety of firms provide service. Super Shuttle is the most popular. It runs every 20 minutes from each terminal. One-way fare to the Big D is $10; the trip takes about 30 minutes; to Ft. Worth it's $18 for the 60 minute trip. During the peak holiday times it's wise to call ahead: (817)-329–2000. Super Shuttles run daily, around the clock.

Car Rentals

Contact car rental agencies by direct phone lines at counters in baggage claim areas. Agencies provide courtesy pick-ups to North/South offices. The only return drop-off is in 5E. On-site agencies are:

Avis	574–4130	Hertz	453–0370
Budget	871–9500	National	1–800–227–7368

Hotel Shuttles

Courtesy phones are located in Baggage Claims areas of each terminal.

Taxis/Limos

Taxis are at all upper-level curbside exits. Fare to Dallas or Ft. Worth is $23. Numerous companies provide both taxi and limo service. For information call 574–5878 or 670–3161.

Parking

All lots charge $.50 for the first hour.
Terminal (Short term): 1–3 hrs./$2, $10/daily maximum.
Long term: 1–3 hrs./$1.50, $5/daily max.
Shuttle lots: 1–3 hrs./$1, $4/daily max.
Buses provide free transport from the shuttle lots. For parking information, call 574-PARK. And if you lose your car (remember this is a *big* complex), call 564–6767. The DFW folks will find it for you. Emergency car care service is available by calling 620–2160.

TRAVELERS SERVICES

DFW boasts 38 snackbars and lounges, 22
newsstands, and numerous specialty shops selling
Tex-gifts,-art, -jewelry,-chocolates,-etc.

Airline Clubs

American's Admiral	3E Gate 33; 2E, Gate 21
Braniff's Business Club	2W Gate 9–10
Delta's Crown (2)	4E (Both clubs)
Piedmont's Presidential Suite	2W Gate 11.
Thai & Air New Zealand VIP Lounge	2W Gate 16.

Baggage Storage

There are 440 coin lockers scattered throughout the
terminals. Rates are $.75 /24 hrs.

Banks

Surprisingly, DFW does not have a full-service bank.
Empire of America ATMs are scattered throughout.
American Express Cash Express machines are located
in 2E, Gate 21, 3E near the American Airlines ticket
counter; and in the 4E Baggage area. DEK Perrera
Currency Exchange has 3 locations: 2E–Gate 21, 2W–
Gate 18, and 4E–Gate 17. Hours vary, depending on
international traffic. Call (214) 979–2411.

Business Services

There is no centralized one-stop service. However, fax
machines are located in Terminal 3E at Gates 27 and
33 newsstands; in Terminal 2E at Gates 10 and 20
newsstands; in Terminal 2W at Gate 9 newsstand; and
in Terminal 4E at Gate 5 newsstand.

Cocktail Lounges

There are at least 20, so if you're a white-knuckler you
have ample opportunity to get fortified. All lounges
close at 11 p.m. State law forbids opening prior to
noon on Sundays. During the week most open at 6
a.m. A domestic beer is $2.50; wine starts at $3.50.

Gift/Specialty Shops

This is the land of the $199 snakeskin boots and $160 sterling silver belt buckles. You can buy gourmet chocolates (Indulgences, 2W), apparel (Texas Gear, Texas Marketplace, both in 2W, The Classic Yellow Rose, 2E), and art (Plush Gallery, 3E).
Benjamin Books has two locations: 3E, Gate 37; and 2W, Gate 4. Open 7 days, 7 a.m.–10 p.m. Remember Jethro Pugh, football fans? If you spot a hulking giant shadowing the shops in the vicinities of 3E, Gate 24, or 2W, Gate 24, that's Jethro. He's part-owner of Pugh's. Jerry Kramer wrote that no one would ever forget a player named Jethro Pugh; we wouldn't dare.

Hotel

The Hyatt-Regency has 1,560 rooms is located on-site. Rates start at $79 during the week; $49 on weekends. Call 453–8400.

Information/Assistance

The Airport Assistance Center functions as a combination information/travelers aid clearinghouse. Staffed around the clock, there is at least one booth in each terminal in the baggage claim area. Call 574–4420.

Military Services

There is no USO. The Airport Assistance Center is the liason information center for military personnel.

Miscellaneous

Barber Shops are in each terminal. A regular cut will run about $12. M–F, 8 to 9 p.m.; Sat. to Sun., 8 a.m. to 6 p.m.
Chapel: There are two, one in 2W, Baggage Claim area; the other in 4E, Gate 2. Call 574–2665.

Post

Drops and stamp vending machines are located in each terminal. DFW also has a 24-hour full-service post office on-site, but it is not readily accessible without vehicular transportation.

Restaurants/Snack Bars

DFW claims to be the largest airport facility in the world, and has more than enough posts of repast. A hot dog is $2.35, sodas are $1.25. Beer is $2.50. The Pizza Strada ($2.50 a slice) is popular. Papaya's in the Hyatt East Tower serves breakfast and lunch buffets.

TIME TO KILL

1 hour . . . The new Delta Satellite Terminal, reached by a 650-foot underground moving sidewalk from 4E offers shops, a cocktail lounge and a restaurant that have unparalleled views of airport operations. A must for "tail watchers."

2 hours . . . Did we mention the dinosaur? Yes and if you want to walk a bit you can see him (or her) on the third level of the Central Utilities Plant which is outside the lower level Hyatt exit. It is best to ask exact directions at the Airport Assistance booths. Tell them you want to see the DFW airport "Watchdog."

3 hours . . . You're tired, frustrated, and slightly "lagged." So take a shower and nap. Air Vita, in the West Tower of the Hyatt, is the ultimate R & R spa for weary travelers. For $5 an hour you can a shower and sleep in a private compartment. Or for $35 you can get a strictly legit massage that leaves you limp—and then for $12 a Norwegian soap-brushing that puts you back together again. Call ahead (214) 574-2026.

4 hours . . . Golf or tennis, anyone? You can play golf on either of the two courses, or tennis (7 courts, including 3 under roof), or racquetball (10 courts) at Hyatt Bear Creek Resort. Greens fees are not unreasonable, starting at $27 plus cart. Clubs and racquets are available for rent. During the week you can usually tee off without waiting. For golf information, call 453-0140; for tennis or racquetball, call 453-0166. Shuttles from the Hyatt to the resort run on demand.

For additional information, call the Dallas Visitors and Convention Center, (214)746-6600

DENVER

STAPLETON INTERNATIONAL AIRPORT

This is a fun airport. There is a relaxed, healthy attitude that prevails here. Passengers wander around with ruddy complexions and smiling faces, holding ski bags. But the people that work here also smile.

Stapleton International Airport was named after Benjamin F. Stapleton, the mayor of Denver in the 1920s. It was opened the same week as the great stock market crash and was soon tagged "Stapleton's Folly" because it was so far away (8 miles) from the city of Denver.

Fifty-seven years later, close to 35 million people mosey on through the "Mile High" city's airport, making Stapleton 5th in passenger traffic in the country. By the year 2000, the FAA projects this western hub will rank number 2. Not bad for being "way out on the prairie."

Despite abundant snowfall and occasional blizzards, Stapleton Airport has been closed only three times for bad weather in its 58-year history—a total of 62 hours and 24 minutes.

The 630 acres originally purchased for Stapleton Airport cost $143,013. Don't forget, this was the beginning of the Great Depression. This same land is now under 15 inches of concrete and the airport has expanded to 4,679 acres.

Stapleton Airport is 5,330 feet above sea level. Go nice and easy on the Tequila Sunrises or John Denver won't be the only one singing about Rocky Mountain highs.

QUICK CONTACTS

Medical Services. . . . 270–1878
Police. . . . 270–1878
Lost & Found. . . . 270–1563
Information. . . . 398–3977 or 1–800–AIR–2–DEN
Paging. . . . 398–3977

THE BASICS

Name: Stapleton International Airport
Airport Code: DEN
Location: 8 miles east of downtown Denver.
Mailing Address: Stapleton International Airport
                 Denver, CO 80207
Telephone: (303) 398–3844
Time: Mountain
Daily Passenger (Rank): 95,000 (5)
Supervising Body: Department of Public Works
                  City/County of Denver

AIRLINE	TELEPHONE	CONCOURSE
Air Midwest	398–5360	D
American	595–9304	C
American West	571–0738	C
Continental	398–3000	C
Continental Commuter	398–3000	A
Continental Express	398–3000	A
Delta	800–221–1212	D
Eastern	398–3333	D
G.P. Express	800–382–6911	A
Northwest Orient	800–225–2525	D
Piedmont	893–3567	D
Trans World	629–7878	D
United	398–4141	B

FINDING YOUR WAY AROUND

Shaped like a scorpion, Stapleton is composed of 6 concourses (A Plus, A, B, C, D, and E). The first level is the baggage claim area and ground transportation services. The second level is ticketing, services and concessions. The third level (Mezzanine) contains offices (including the Aviation Historical Society) and other services. International Arrivals are at Concourse C-2.

INFORMATION FOR THE HANDICAPPED

DEN conforms to standards provided by the Architectural and Transportation Barriers Compliance Board for elderly and handicapped travelers. We emphasize notifying the airline you are traveling with ahead of time if you need special assistance. TDD's are located in two areas: Travelers Aid (Great Hall area) and Airport Security (mezzanine between concourses C and D).

GROUND TRANSPORTATION

All ground transportation services are located on Level 1 (baggage area). A Consolidated Ground Transportation desk is located on level 1 (inside door 6) and staffed to assist travelers with information and arrangements. Transportation vehicles load in the South Shuttle Lot (purple line outside door 2) or the North Shuttle Lot (purple line outside door 9). For additional information call 270–1750.

Airport Shuttles

Airline: Access to A Plus Concourse (Gates A15 & A16) by shuttle bus only. Pick-up at either end of the central terminal area, lower level.
Blue and white (SMART) buses pick passengers up every 15 minutes at designated parking lots and take them to the terminal (free).
Shuttle Parking Lot # 2—42nd & Ulster
Shuttle Parking Lot # 3—26th & Syracruse
Hotels: Courtesy phones are located at Level 1 (baggage area).

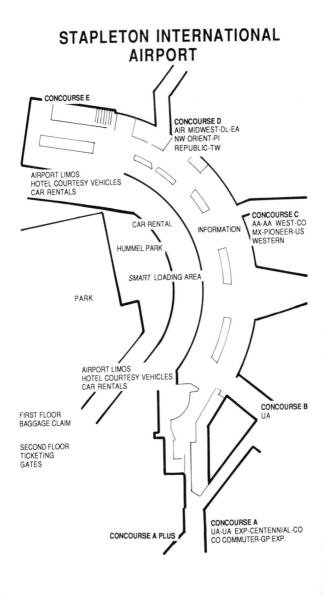

STAPLETON INTERNATIONAL AIRPORT

CONCOURSE E

CONCOURSE D
AIR MIDWEST-DL-EA
NW ORIENT-PI
REPUBLIC-TW

AIRPORT LIMOS
HOTEL COURTESY VEHICLES
CAR RENTALS

CONCOURSE C
AA-AA WEST-CO
MX-PIONEER-US
WESTERN

CAR RENTAL

INFORMATION

HUMMEL PARK

SMART LOADING AREA

PARK

AIRPORT LIMOS
HOTEL COURTESY VEHICLES
CAR RENTALS

CONCOURSE B
UA

FIRST FLOOR
BAGGAGE CLAIM

SECOND FLOOR
TICKETING
GATES

CONCOURSE A
UA-UA EXP-CENTENNIAL-CO
CO COMMUTER-GP EXP.

CONCOURSE A PLUS

DENVER AREA

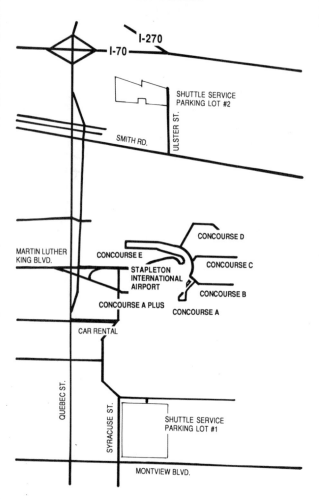

Vehicles pick up in North and South Shuttle Lots (ground level).

Buses

RTD Buses: Depart from the north end of the terminal drive (across doors 5–7). Schedule information at the bus stop and the ground transportation booth (door 7).

Trailways and Grey Line: Information and rates, Trailways booth, baggage claim area.

Charter Buses: Located in the South Shuttle lot, level 1. Purple line outside door 2 (baggage claim area).

Car Rentals

Scattered among the information counters (baggage claim area) are the car rental companies.

Avis	398–3725	Hertz	355–2244
Budget	399–0444	National	321–7990
Dollar	398–2323		

Taxis/Limos

Taxis: Outside doors 4, 6, 10 (baggage area). $8/one way to downtown area.

Limos: Limos load in North & South Shuttle Lots (ground level).

Parking

The airport terminal parking is located on the 3rd level with pedestrian walks to terminal building. Parking for the first half-hour is free. Parking Information: for space available call 398-CARS or radio AM530; for emergency call 398–3814.

Close In: $1/second half-hr., $1/each additional hour
$7/each 24 hr. period.

Short Term: $1/second half-hr.
$.50/each additional half-hr.

Shuttle Service Parking: Lots 2 & 3 (see Buses)
$1/each hr.
$3/each 24 hr. period.

TRAVELERS SERVICES

Certainly the flavor of the cosmopolitan West is present at Stapleton. From restaurants called "Timberline" and "Cantina" (serving Mexican and Southwestern specialties) to shops featuring gifts from Spain, Mexico, South America and the Orient. Don't miss the Ice Cream Works or the Candy and Popcorn Store. They're irresistible!

Airline Clubs

American's Admiral	E-6
Continental's President	A-16, C-19
Delta's Crown	3rd floor (Mezzanine)
TWA's Ambassador	D 5–7
United's Red Carpet	B-3

Baggage Storage

The storage Room is located across from Door #3, baggage claim level. Open daily, 6:30 a.m. to 11 p.m.
$2/item—24 hrs.
$4/oversized item—24 hrs.
Lockers—all concourses—$1/24 hrs.

Banks

Ace Cash Express:
Located in the Main Terminal (ticket level). Open 7 days, 7 a.m. to 7 p.m.
Automated Teller Machines (ATM): Located in the Main Terminal (across from the Timberline Restaurant).
Travelers Insurance and Foreign Currency Exchange: Main Terminal.

Business Services

Travelers may use fax in Administration Office (3rd floor) M–F, 8 a.m. to 5 p.m.

Cocktail Lounges

Unless you are a teetotaler, cocktail lounges named Mountain Greenery (entrance to Concourse D), Trail Ridge (D-25), Silverspur (D-9) and (pay attention ski fanatics) Schuss Bar (B-5) are bound to be inviting.

Additional lounges are located throughout the airport and most are open from 7 a.m. to 10 a.m.

Gift Shops/Newsstands

All concourses. Specialty carts with unique gifts are located on the connector bridge between A, B & E concourses. For the sweet tooth, try Stephany's Candy Store. The candy is homemade and delicious. Recommendation: Either the "Denver Mint" or "Colorado Almond Toffee." Both have received the seal of excellence from the Colorado State Fair.

Hotels

No on-site hotel. Hotel courtesy phones are located in the baggage claim area.

Information/Assistance

Information counters (4) are located on the second level, Concourse B, C, D & E, and staffed with service representatives, 6:30 a.m. to 10 p.m., 7 days a week. There is also an information booth on the first level (baggage area).
Travelers Aid—Main Terminal: Call 398–3873.

Military Services

USO, third floor (Mezzanine), B & C Concourse. 8 a.m. to 9 p.m. Call 398–2288.

Miscellaneous

Barbershop: Main Terminal (Mezzanine)
Chapel: Across from the military lounge (3rd floor).
          Obtain key from Stapleton operator.
Flower carts: No permanent location.
Game Room: Main Terminal (Ticket Level)
Nursery: Located next to the military lounge, Main
          Terminal (3rd floor) Obtain key from
          Travelers Aid.
Shoeshine: Main Terminal (Baggage Level)

Post

Full service facility-baggage area-Door # 2;
9 a.m. to 5 p.m. M–F, 9 a.m. to midnight Sat.

Restaurants/Snack Bars

There is a great selection of food here. Even the
snacks are mouth-watering. If you want elegant
dining, try the Signature Room. *Fortune* magazine has
selected it as the best restaurant in any airport.
Offering continental cuisine, it is open for lunch
11 a.m. to 2 p.m. or for dinner, 4 p.m. to 9 p.m. Or
do you yearn for something spicier? Try Cantina. It
serves Mexican and Southwestern specialties. Want a
delicious snack? Try homemade ice cream from the
Ice Cream Works.

TIME TO KILL

1 hour. . . . Well, if you ski or have ever fantasized
being on the slopes, you can ride the escalator down
to the baggage area, and across from door #3 you will
find the best information on skiing in Colorado. Free.

Or. . . . Walk into the Main Terminal area and gaze
up at the Curtiss JN-4 Jenny. Built in 1918, this
vintage airplane permanently soars in the Great Hall
area.

2 hours. . . . Denver's Museum of Natural History is
the second largest in the country, just behind
Washington, D.C.'s. It is only 20 minutes away,
round-trip. Open 9 a.m. to 5 p.m. daily. Admission:
$4/adults and $2/children and senior citizens. 370–
6363. Gates Planetarium is part of the museum and
offers a celestial view. Open T–Sun. Admission: $3/
adults and $3/children and senior citizens. Show
times vary, so call ahead: 370–6351.

3 hours. . . . Rain, snow or shine, it makes no
difference at the Denver Botanical Gardens. An entire
jungle of tropical and subtropical plants grow in
indoor and outdoor environs. Open
9 a.m. to 4:45 p.m. Admission: $3/adults. Call
331–4010.

Or. . . . Take a free tour of the Denver Mint. It's only
15 minutes from the airport and you'll be humming
"Goldfinger." The Denver Mint houses the second
largest gold reserve in the country; Fort Knox is No.

1. The tours run 20 minutes and are scheduled at 30 minute intervals. Open Monday 9:30 a.m. to 3 p.m. and T–F, 8:30 a.m. to 3 p.m. Call 844–3582.

4 hours. . . . Be a kid again! Go to the City Park Zoo. With over 1,550 critters, including Bengal tigers, polar and grizzly bears, you won't get lonely. Open daily 10 a.m. to 5 p.m. Admission: $4/adults and $2/children and senior citizens. If you're under 6, it's free. Call 331–4110.

For additional information visit Denver's visitor's bureau in the Great Hall area between concourses C and D or call the Denver Convention and Visitors Bureau (303) 892–1112.

DETROIT

DETROIT METROPOLITAN WAYNE COUNTY AIRPORT

Detroit Metro has shown dramatic growth since airline deregulation in 1978. In the last seven years, passenger volume has more than doubled, going from 9 million in 1982 to over 19 million in 1987. As a consequence, Detroit Metro has embarked on a $450 million capital improvement plan. More runways and taxiways, more sophisticated air traffic control equipment and terminal expansions are all part of the plan.

DTW's terminals are named for individuals: Leroy Smith, James Davey, and Michael Berry. Until 1985 DTW was managed by the Board of Road Commissioners and all three of those men served on the Board at one time.

DTW was the nation's first designated inland commercial jetport when the Smith Terminal opened in 1958.

That huge jet and advertising slogan you see on the Northwest Airlines hanger is reputedly the world's largest hand-painted sign. It was executed in 1985.

QUICK CONTACTS

Medical . . . 942–3600
Police . . . 942–3681
Lost & Found . . . 942–3669
Information . . . 942–3550
Paging . . . Airlines Only

THE BASICS

Name: Detroit Metropolitan Wayne County Airport
Airport Code: DTW
Location: 23 miles southwest of Detroit
Mailing Address: Detroit Metropolitan Wayne Co.
                Airport
                L. C. Smith Terminal
                Detroit, MI 48242
Telephone: (313) 942–3550
Time: Eastern
Daily Passengers (Rank): 54,101 (18)
Supervising Body: Wayne County Division of
                Airports

AIRLINE	TELEPHONE	CONCOURSE
Air Canada	833–3200	Berry
American	965–1000	B
Braniff	1–800–272–9297	A
British Airways	1–800–247–9297	Berry
Continental	963–4600	B
Delta	355–3200	C
Delta/Comair	355–3200	C
Eastern	965–8200	B
Midway	1–800–621–5700	C
Midwest Express	1–800–452–2022	A
Northwest	962–2002	D,E,F,G
NW Airlink	962–2002	G
PanAm	1–800–221–1111	Berry
Piedmont	962–8765	B
Southwest	562–1221	A
TWA	962–8650	C
United	336–9000	A
USAir	963–8340	C

FINDING YOUR WAY AROUND

DTW consists of three terminals: Smith, with
concourses A, B, and C; Davey, concourses F and G;
and Berry International Terminal. Concourses D and
E are between Smith and Davey. Moving sidewalks
connect Smith and Davey; shuttle vans to Berry run

every seven minutes. The Marriott Hotel is between Smith and Davey.

INFORMATION FOR THE HANDICAPPED

DTW offers facilities for handicapped and elderly travelers in accordance with standards provided by the Architectural and Transportation Barriers Compliance Board. All airports emphasize that travelers with special needs should make prior arrangements with their airlines. TDD units are available at the Travelers Aid booth.

GROUND TRANSPORTATION

All ground transportation services depart from the baggage claims areas in each of the three terminals.

Buses

Commuter Trans Vans run every 30 minutes beginning at 6:45 a.m. until 6:15 p.m., weekdays. On the weekends they run every hour beginning at 7 a.m. until 11 p.m. One-way fare to downtown is $11.

Car Rentals

Rental counters are in all three terminals for the following agencies:

Avis	1–800–331–1212	Hertz	729–5200
Budget	326–6880	National	941–7000
Dollar	942–1905		

Hotel Shuttles

Courtesy phones are located in the baggage claims area of each terminal.

Taxis/Limos

The fare to downtown is $29. Pickups are in front of the hotel.
Carey Limo provides service throughout Metro area. Call 1–800–336–4646. Fare to downtown is $120.

Parking

Short term lots: $1.50/half-hr, $24/daily max; Main, West, and International lots: $2/1st hr, $4/daily max.

Deck lots: $2.75/1st hour; $6/daily max:
Long term lot: $3.25 flat rate per 24 hours.
Free shuttles to all lots run every 10 minutes.

TRAVELERS SERVICES

DTW lacks the updated travelers amenities of newer
airport facilities.

Airline Clubs

American's Admiral	Smith Terminal, Mezzanine Level
Delta's Crown	Between D and E Concourses
Northwest's World Club	Between D and E Concourses Concourse F, Davey Terminal
Pan Am's Clipper	International Terminal

Baggage Storage

Coin lockers are located on each concourse and
charge $.75/day.

Banks

Comerica Bank is located in the Davey Terminal.
Hours: M–Th, 9 a.m. to noon; F, 9:30 a.m. to noon,
1:30 p.m. to 4 p.m. Each terminal also has an ATM.
American Express Cash Express is in the Smith
Terminal. Foreign currency exchanges are in the
Mutual of Omaha Service Centers, in Comerica Bank,
and in the International Terminal.

Business Services

Mutual of Omaha operates two service centers, one
each in the Smith and Davey Terminals. Hours are
daily, 6 a.m. to 9 p.m. Services include word
processing, fax, notary, and copying.

Cocktail Lounges

There are 10 lounges throughout DTW. Opening
hours vary. Most stay open until 11 p.m.

Gift Shops/Newsstands

There are seven gift shops and six newsstands that provide basic travelers services.

Hotel

Marriott operates a 162-room hotel between the Smith and Davey Terminals. Weekday rates start at $105, weekend rates, $55. Call 941–9400.

Information/Assistance

Booths are located in all three terminals and are staffed daily from 7 a.m. to 10 p.m. Call 942–3550 Travelers Aid has locations in the baggage claims areas of the Smith Terminal and Davey Terminal. Hours daily, 9 a.m. to 9 p.m. Call 942–6740.

Miscellaneous

Barbershops: Located in the Smith and the Davey Terminals. Open daily, 7 a.m.–8 p.m.
Christian Science Reading Room: Located on the mezzanine level of the Smith Terminal.
Nursery/Changing Room: Smith Terminal.
Video Arcade: Smith Terminal. Open 24 hours.

Post

A full-service post office is located near the Delta ticket counters in the Smith Terminal. Hours M–F, 8:30 to noon, 1 a.m. to 4:30 p.m. Stamp vending machines and mail drops are scattered throughout the airport.

Restaurants/Snack Bars

Six restaurants, most decorated with a sports motif, and 10 snack bars are located throughout the complex, where a cheeseburger platter costs $5.95; soup of the day, $3.25. At least one snackbar in each terminal is open 24 hours. The Innkeeper near the C Concourse is DTW's full-service restaurant.

TIME TO KILL

DTW offers few amenities for the delayed traveler, and the lack of rapid transit makes journeying off-site time-consuming and expensive. If you're only here two hours this is the time to catch up on your reading. But, if you have the time, try:

3 hours . . . The Cultural Center in downtown Detroit is a neighborhood of art and history museums and a science center. Open T–Sun, 9 a.m. to 5 p.m. Admission is free, except for the Science Center which is $4. Call 577–5088.

4 hours . . . If this is your one shot at Detroit, a must-see is the Greenfield Village/Henry Ford Museum complex in Dearborn. Both are open daily, 9 a.m. to 5 p.m. The Village is a 240-acre working farm and includes reconstructions of the birthplaces of Ford, Harvey Firestone, Daniel Webster, plus Thomas Edison's Menlo Park laboratory which was moved nails and all from New Jersey. Admission to either the Village or the Ford Museum is $9.50. Call 271–1620.

For additional information call the Detroit Visitors Center, 567–1170, or the 24-hour events line, 298–6262.

HONOLULU

HONOLULU
INTERNATIONAL AIRPORT

As you pass through the open walkways that connect each terminal, warm breezes gently welcome you to Hawaii. An open concept (only the holding rooms are air-conditioned), Honolulu International Airport feels carefree and very tropical.

HNL is approximately 4 miles from downtown and 8 miles from the famous Waikiki beach, but if you arrive during the morning or evening rush hour the 4 or 8 seems more like 40.

Hawaii's first commercial airport, HNL was originally named after Pacific pioneer aviator, John Rogers, a navy commander noted for a daring transPacific flight from San Francisco to Hawaii in 1925 (2 years before Charles Lindbergh flew solo across the Atlantic).

In 1935, Pan American Airways inaugurated the first commercial flight from the Mainland to Hawaii. It took 17 hours and 14 minutes from San Francisco to Pearl Harbor. Fifty-four years later, the same flight takes 12 hours and 50 minutes. The flight time has been reduced by 5 hours and 36 minutes because of the 6 hour layover in Los Angeles. Progress.

The world's first major offshore runway was constructed at HNL. The reef runway is 12,357 feet long.

To get your bearings Hawaiian-style—when you are flying into Honolulu Airport you are flying Mauka or toward the mountain. When you are leaving Honolulu you are flying Makai or toward the ocean. And whether you are coming or going it is still Aloha.

QUICK CONTACTS

Medical 833–3445
Police 836–6411
Lost & Found 836–6440
Information 836–6413
Paging . . . . Airlines

THE BASICS

Name: Honolulu International Airport
Airport Code: HNL
Location: Island of Oahu. 3,859 air miles from San
Francisco, 7,997 air miles from New York.
Mailing Address: Terminal Box No. 4
Honolulu, Hawaii 96819
Telephone: (808) 836–6411
Time: 5 hour time difference from the East coast.
Daily Passenger (Rank): 55,791 (15)
Supervising Body: State of Hawaii
Department of Transportation

AIRLINE	TELEPHONE	LOCATION
Air America	834–7172	C
Air Micronesia	1–800–231–0856	C
Air New Zealand	1–800–521–4059	C
Aloha	836–1111	COM
American	526–0044	C
Canadian	922–0533	C
China	836–1052	C
Continental	1–800–231–0856	D
Delta	1–800–221–1212	C
Hawaiian	537–5100	C
Japan	836–5151	C
Mid-Pacific	836–3313	I
Korean	836–1711	C
Northwest	995–2255	M
Pan Am	1–800–221–1111	EWA
Philippine	536–1928	C
Princeville	833–3219	D
Qantas	836–2461	EWA
Singapore	836–0375	C
TWA	1–800–221–2000	C

AIRLINE	TELEPHONE	LOCATION
United	547–2211	D
Wardair	995–5981	C

(C-Central or Overseas, COM-Commuter, M-Main, E-EWA, D-Diamond)

FINDING YOUR WAY AROUND

Honolulu Airport is comprised of a Main Terminal (multi-level) and three appendaged concourses; Diamond Head, Central, and Ewa. The Central concourse serves as the overseas main terminal. An Inter-Island Terminal adjoins the Main Terminal on the western end of the complex. The lower level of the terminal complex contains the baggage claim area and transportation services. The upper levels are for ticketing/check-in and amenities such as shops and restaurants.

INFORMATION FOR THE HANDICAPPED

HNL follows the standards set by the Architectural and Transportation Compliance Board for handicapped and elderly travelers. For special assistance, notify your airline ahead of time. For additional information, call 836–6413. A brochure for disabled passengers describing specific airport services and facilities is available at information counters. TDD's are located in the Central Terminal lobby.

GROUND TRANSPORTATION

All transportation services are located on the ground level. An Airporter bus provides transportation to Waikiki or a city bus is also available. A taxi to the downtown area will run about $8 and takes at least 30 minutes; to Waikiki, about $14. Your best bet is to catch one of the limo services and that will only cost $3.50 to $4 to Waikiki, where all the hotels and shops are located. The city bus also operates from the airport to Waikiki and it's cheap—$.60. No luggage is allowed unless you can fit it on your lap.

Airport Shuttles

Free shuttle transportation (Wiki Wiki) is provided between the Main Terminal, the Ewa Concourse, Diamond Head Concourse and the Inter-Island Concourse. The shuttles to the gates are boarded on the upper level of the Main Terminal. An additional shuttle service is provided between the Main Terminal, the Commuter Terminal and the Inter-Island Terminal.

Buses

The Airporter Bus is located on the lower level near the baggage claim area. The designated stops are # 16, 27, 32, and 38. It runs from 6:30 a.m. to 9:45 p.m. Fare to Waikiki: $5/one way. Luggage is allowed but limited to 2 suitcases and 1 carry-on. Call 926-4747. The city bus (TheBUS) is located on the upper level in front of the Main Terminal. It runs from 7 a.m. to 9 p.m. Fare to Waikiki: $.60/adults, one way, $.25/children. Luggage is not allowed unless it can fit under your seat. Call 531-1611.
The Airporter and the city buses are also located at the Inter-Island Terminal (near baggage claim area A).

Car Rentals

Car rentals are located on the ground level of the Main Terminal and at the Inter-Island Terminal.

Alamo	833-4585	National	836-2655
Avis	834-5564	Rent Rite	834-1016
Budget	836-1700	Thrifty	836-2388
Dollar	831-2330	USA	526-9939
Hertz	836-2691		

Hotel Shuttles

Hotel telephones for hotel shuttles are located across from the car rentals in the main terminal.

Taxis/Limos

Taxis: Airport to downtown. $8/person.

Limos: Airport to downtown. $3.50 to $4/person.

Carey Limousine	836–1422
Elite Limousine	735–2431
Dav El Limousine	800–922–0343
Silver Cloud Limo	524–7999

Parking

A multi-level parking garage faces the Main Terminal complex. Public parking in open lots is available on either side of the parking garage. Rates: $.50/30 min. $.75 ea. additional hr. $7 day, max./24 hrs. Call 836–1355.

TRAVELERS SERVICES

Services at HNL include a barbershop, a shoeshine, a currency exchange, and shower/sleep facilities. For those of you in transit from an international flight the arrival hours are usually very early or very late. There is a 24-hour coffee shop on the second level of the Main Terminal to accommodate the bleary-eyed.

Airline Clubs

Air New Zealand	Main Terminal, ground level
Aloha	Inter-Island Terminal
American's Admiral	Main Terminal, ground level
China's Dynasty	Main Terminal, ground level
Continental's Presidents	Main Terminal, ground level
Canadian's Maple Leaf	Main Terminal, ground level
Delta's Crown Room	Main Terminal, ground level
Hawaiian	Inter-Island Terminal
Japan's Sakura	Main Terminal, second level
Korean's First Class Lounge	Main Terminal, ground level
Northwest's World Club	Main Terminal, second level

Philippine's Mabuhau	Main Terminal, ground level
Qantas' Captain	Main Terminal, second level
Singapore's Silver Cris	Main Terminal, third level
United's Red Carpet	Main Terminal, third level

Baggage Storage

Baggage Storage and Lost & Found are located in the mall area (ground level—western end of the Main Terminal). Lockers are located throughout the ground transportation area (mall) in the Main Terminal.

Banks

Bank of Hawaii: Full service bank. Call 538–4818. M—Th, 8:30 a.m. to 3 p.m. F–8:30 a.m. to 6 p.m.
Deak International, Ltd. Currency Exchange. Call 834–1099.
Located at the following 4 locations:
Main Office (main lobby) 8:15 a.m. to 4 p.m. 834–1099.
EWA Counter (near duty free) 8:15 a.m. to 4 p.m. 836–5893.
Diamond Head Counter (near gate #13) 7:15 a.m. to 3 p.m. 833–2672.
International Arrivals (In/Out) 6:15 a.m. to 2 p.m. 833–4745.
An ATM machine is located near the United ticketing counter (West end of the Main Terminal).

Business Services

Conference/banquet rooms are available for airport-related business only.

Cocktail Lounges

Cocktail lounges are located in all terminals.

Gift Shops/Newsstands

There are duty-free shops for those traveling internationally, a variety of gift shops offering island products including the alluring fragrant leis. Note: As you drive into the airport the lei stands are less expensive but even the leis at the airport are reasonable ($6 and up). Macadamia nuts whether purchased here or on the Mainland are high.

Information/Assistance

Flight information monitors are located in the ticket lobbies and waiting areas. Fifteen visitor Information counters are located throughout the airport. A central information desk is located in the main lobby area on the second level. Program hosts and hostesses can assist travelers in 10 languages including Ilocano and Samoan.

Military Services

USO: Second Level, Main Terminal

Miscellaneous

Shower: The Shower Tree is a shower/sleep facility located on the second level of the Main Terminal. Rates: $7.50/shower, which includes all toiletries, $2.25/shave, $3/hr. for sleeping facilities or $18/8 hrs. with a shower. Open 24 hours. Call 836–3044.

Post

Mail drops and stamp machines are available throughout all concourses and terminals. A post office is located right outside the airport's east side.

Restaurant/Snack Bars

There is a 24-hour coffee shop on the second level of the main lobby area and a full-service restaurant (Garden Top) serving island specialties as well as continental cuisine. M–Th, 11 a.m. to 10 p.m., and F–Sun, 10 a.m. to 10 p.m. There are additional food concessions and snack bars throughout the airport complex.

TIME TO KILL

1 hour . . . Definitely see the Gardens. Take your pick. Hawaiian, Chinese or Japanese. Translated: a beautiful and relaxing way to unwind after a long journey. All three are located in the lower level of the Main Terminal near Gates 14 to 23.

2 hours . . . How can you pass up an opportunity to shop? Unless you hit this airport at the odd hour, it is fun to just browse looking at some of the Island wares. Leis are famous here, and they are conveniently packaged and are not that expensive. They are also fun to receive.

3 hours . . . The downtown area is only 4 miles away and if you don't hit rush hour a bus ride into town should only take 20 minutes. TheBUS is inexpensive (\$.60) and goes everywhere. Once you are there you have a wealth of attractions to choose from (most of them you can't pronounce) like Iolani Palace, Kawaiahao Church, the statue of King Kamehameha; or you may just want to take in the sights from the bus. Recommended: for some Hawaiian history, the Bishop Museum is an excellent choice. It is open daily from 9 a.m. to 5 p.m. Admission: \$4.75. Call 847–3511.

4 hours or more . . . Take a Pearl Harbor cruise. It includes a 3-hour narrative on Pearl Harbor and you will visit the Arizona Memorial and other points of interest. Adults: \$10, Children: \$5. Call 536–3641.

If it's on your wish list, you can catch a bus and in forty minutes (unless you hit rush hour) be at Waikiki, crowded with hotels and motels and people. Fight your way to the beach (it really is there, somewhere), sniff the salt air and with your imagination in full gear, imagine Michener's Hawaii.

For additional information call the Hawaii Visitor Information Center, (808) 836–6413.

HOUSTON

HOUSTON INTERCONTINENTAL AIRPORT

In 1937, the city of Houston acquired its first public airport. It was dedicated as "Houston Municipal Airport." After several years and several names (including Howard Hughes) it became the William P. Hobby airport in 1967 in honor of the former Governor of Texas. Two years later, in response to burgeoning growth generated by erupting oil wells, a new airport was built 22 miles north of the city—Houston Intercontinental Airport.

Although Houston is the fourth most populated city in the U.S., IAH only ranks twenty-seventh in passenger traffic in the world, just under Philadelphia and barely ahead of Orlando. It is a modern and well designed facility, with a subway system developed by Disney World that quickly and efficiently moves the masses. A passenger can travel from Terminal A to Terminal C in 6 minutes. So if you want to get off at Terminal B you better think fast.

The "Hughes Airport" name didn't set well with the bureaucrats in Washington. It seems you can't name an airport after a living person if you want federal funds.

QUICK CONTACTS
Medical 230–3111
Police 230–3111
Lost & Found 230–3100
Information 230–3100
Paging 230–3000

THE BASICS

Name: Houston Intercontinental Airport
Airport Code: IAH
Location: 22 miles north of downtown Houston
Mailing Address: PO Box 60106
                 Houston, TX 77205
Telephone: (713) 230–3100
Time: Central
Daily Passengers (Rank): 42,161 (19)
Supervising Body: City of Houston

AIRLINE	TELEPHONES	LOCATION
Aero Mexico	691–3071	B
Air France	1–800–221–2110	B
American Airlines	222–9873	B
Aviateca	442–9927	B
British Airways	445–3501	B
Cayman Airways	1–800–327–2864	B
Continental	780–3344	C
Continental Express	780–3344	C
Delta	623–6000	B
KLM	1–800–777–5553	B
Lufthansa	1–800–645–3882	B
Northwest	868–9988	A
Piedmont	757–9707	A
Southwest	237–1221	A
TACA	864–9985	B
SAHSA	683–7177	B
TWA	222–7273	B
United	650–1055	A
USAir	1–800–428–4322	A
VIASA	1–800–327–5454	C

FINDING YOUR WAY AROUND

Described as a "city within a city," Houston
Intercontinental is designed like a mall. There are 3
terminals (A, B, and C) with a Marriott Airport Hotel
located in the center of the complex. All the terminals
and the hotel are linked by an automated subway
system. Each terminal has its own parking area with
ground transportation facilities located on the street

level. A perimeter drive serves all 3 terminals and the hotel. The second level is comprised of airline ticket counters, concessions and other amenities. The third level is used for parking.

Houston's International Terminal is located in Terminal B. Passengers in transit can wait in comfort in the Intransit Lounge (capacity for 200) with food and beverage service available. There is also a currency exchange facility opened during the hours of scheduled international flights.

INFORMATION FOR THE HANDICAPPED

This airport provides facilities for the handicapped and elderly, in accordance with standards set by the Architectural and Transportation Barriers Compliance Board. TDD's are located in the following Terminals:

Terminal A: Upper level, Toward Gates A16–20.
Terminal B: Upper level, Toward Gates B16–20.
Terminal C: First Aid Station

GROUND TRANSPORTATION

All ground transportation services are available at street level with taxis, limos and public transport exiting from one doorway (south) and private vehicle pickup through another (north). The least expensive fare downtown is the Airport Express or to share a cab. It takes approximately 45 to 60 minutes.

Buses

Airport Express: 523–8888. It departs from all the terminals (baggage claim area). It operates daily from 6:50 a.m. to 1:00 a.m. Fare: $7.95/person.

Hotel Shuttles

Courtesy phones are available at the north side of each terminal (baggage claim area).

Taxis/Limos

Taxis: Fare to downtown is $22.50/person. Yellow Cab offers discount rates to Share-A-Ride. Fares: $11.25/ 2 passengers, $7.50/ 3 passengers and $5.63/ 4 passengers.

Limos: Stagecoach Airport Limousine—242-3994
Airport Limousine—785-5258
Additional limousine services are available.

Car Rentals

Car rental counters are located in each of the
terminals across from the baggage claim areas.

Airways	447-1074	General	446-4670
Alamo	590-5100	Hertz	443-8000
Avis	443-5800	National	443-8850
Budget	944-1888	Payless	590-6188
Dollar	449-0161	Snappy	590-6188
Enterprise	540-1451	Thrifty	442-5000

Parking

Each terminal is equipped with garage parking and
additional close surface parking. There is also an
economy parking lot with free shuttle service. Parking
meters are available in all terminals: airside, 10 min./
$.25 and surface lot, 12 min./$.25
Terminal Parking: All terminals: all levels
0–1.5 hrs./$2, 1.5–2.5 hrs./$3, 2.5–5 hrs./$4, 5–24 hrs./
$5
Surface Lots: Areas 2 and 4
0–1.5 hrs./$2, 1.5–2.5 hrs./$3, 2.5–24 hrs./$4
Economy Parking: 0–24 hrs./$3

TRAVELERS SERVICES

Most travelers services are located on the second level
of all terminals. Included in the airport complex and
connected by subway is the Hotel Marriott. It offers a
restaurant, a cafe, a gift shop, a barber/beauty shop
and a boutique in addition to hotel rooms.

Airline Clubs

All clubs are on the mezzanine level unless otherwise
indicated

Air France	Terminal B
British Airways	Terminal B

(Presently using KLM's lounge until their Clipper
Lounge is renovated).

Continental's 1st Class Lounge	Terminal C (South Concourse, near gates C34-C41).
Continental's Young Traveler's Club	Terminal C (South Concourse, near gates C-42-C45).
President's Club	Terminal C
Delta's Crown Room	Terminal B
KLM's Rembrandt Room	Terminal B
KLM's Business Class	Terminal B (entrance of Flight Station 6).
Lufthansa's 1st class Lounge	Terminal B (shares with Delta).

Baggage Storage

Lockers are available in all terminals. Rate: $.50/day.

Banks

No full service banks are available.
ATMs: Terminals A and B

Business Services

None available.

Cocktail Lounges

Cocktail lounges are available in each terminal and in the Hotel Marriott. Some of the lounges have mouth-watering seafood bars.

Gift Shops/Newsstands

This is not the Galleria—not even close. Houston's Intercontinental offers run-of-the-mill airport shopping. If you are interested in taking back a bit of Texas, Avis Boots (North Concourse, Terminal C) sells a popular item—The Charley-1-Horse hat (JR of Dallas and RR formerly of Washington, D.C. wear them). Although the hat's namesake hailed from the West the hats are made in Chicago. They start at $150.

Hotel

The Marriott Hotel is located between Terminals B and C. It is 7 floors high and has 566 rooms; you can wrangle a single or double on a weekend for about $75. Weekdays a single or double will cost you $98. If you want a room for 1 hour up to 8 hours, the fee is $40 an hour. Rooms by the hour are only available from 8 a.m. to 6 p.m. For reservations call 443–2310.

Information/Assistance

On level 1 of each terminal is a Visitors Information Center. On level 2 of each terminal is an information booth.

Traveler's Aid counters are located in every terminal and are staffed from 9 a.m. to 8 p.m. After hours, call 668–0911.

Military Services

USO: Terminal C, North Concourse, west end, just before entering Gates C4–C-12.

Miscellaneous

Barber/Beauty Shop: Airport's Marriott Hotel (lobby level). Open M–Sat ., 7 a.m. to 6 p.m. Take the interterminal subway train.
Game Room: Terminals A and B (lobby level). Terminal C (North & South Concourse). Open 24 hours.
Pay TV: Each terminal, $.25/15 min.
Shoe Shine: Terminals A and B (lobby level), Terminal C (North Concourse).
Chapel: Terminal C, Second Level, south end.
Nursery: Terminal A, Second Level, north end near Gates A1–5, Terminal B, Second Level, north end near Gates B1–5, Terminal C, Second Level, south end

Post

A post office is located outside airport and stamp vending machines and mail drops are located in all the terminals.

Restaurants

Buffeterias are located in all the terminals. A salad bar and pizza parlor are located in Terminal C, North Concourse. CK's is the restaurant atop the Hotel Marriott. It serves continental cuisine and is open: M–F, 11:30 a.m. to 2:30 p.m., and from 5:30 p.m. to Midnight. Sat, 5:30 p.m. to 10 p.m. Sun, 11 a.m. to 3 p.m.

A Sunday brunch is served complete with champagne. The cost is $15.95 for adults, and $5.95 for children. The bubbly is poured after noon. Call for dinner reservations: 443–2310.

TIME TO KILL

1 hour. . . . Gauntlet, Zelda, Double Dragon, Mario & Luigi—if any of this makes sense then we don't have to tell you how to kill your hour. Every terminal has two video game rooms.

2 hours. . . . Dine at CK's, the revolving restaurant high in the sky at the hotel tower. Enjoy continental cuisine with a view. One hour and 360 degrees later you will have viewed Houston in the round.

3 hours. . . . We're afraid you're still at the airport. Not much to do here. Hope you brought a book.

4 hours or more. . . . Everything is bigger, better and further in Texas. Remember the airport is 22 miles from downtown so schedule 1 hour, one way. The Airport Express is our choice. It is reasonable in fare and it runs frequently. Even if you ride the bus just to see Houston's skyline; it's worth it. Huge, towering, glass structures grow before your eyes as you approach this city of megabucks.

Visit the Museum of Fine Arts, a museum housing antiquities to modern art. T–Sat, 10 a.m. to 5 p.m., Sun, noon to 5 p.m. Admission: $2. Call 639–7300.

Catty-corner to the Museum of Fine Arts is the Contemporary Art Museum. A borrowing museum, the art comes and goes. Exhibits feature art by Warhol, Jasper John, Rauschenberg, etc. The finest of twentieth century art is at your disposal, free. Hours: T–Sat. 10 a.m. to 5 p.m. and Sun. noon to 6 p.m. Call 526–3129 (recording). Free.

The Astro-Complex includes the Astrodome (sports events), the Astrohall (auto and boat shows, home shows, etc.), and the Astroworld Theme Park (Amusement Park). Call 799–1234.

For the fun of it: Beneath the glass, brick, stone and steel lies an underground network of tunnels connecting 4 miles of buildings. So if the streets look vacant, it could be that the "suits" are walking down-under. Where do you enter? Most major buildings have access but the Hyatt Regency in the downtown area and the Park Shopping mall at San Jacinto and McKinney are open on weekends. There are shops below but they only stay open on weekdays.

For additional information contact the Greater Houston Convention and Visitors Bureau (713) 523–5050 or 1–800–231–7799.

KANSAS CITY

KANSAS CITY
INTERNATIONAL AIRPORT

This is a "no frills" airport, expressing the hardworking and honest values you would expect on the prairie. But don't be fooled by MCI's lack of urbanity. It is one of the best: easy to get around with good signage, and downright convenient. Its three self-contained, round terminals bob like doughnuts amid the buffalo grass of the rolling Missouri countryside. This configuration, unique in the 1972 dedication year, has been much imitated since. MCI is also an example of prescient planning. Besides coming in slightly under its $250 million budget, the facility is virtually unchanged in 16 years. Even today, MCI operates at less than 75 percent of planned capacity although it has maintained a steady and healthy growth rate.

Officially it's "MCI," but popularly it's known as "KCI." Tagged with the name of Mid-Continent International back during the design stage, the code stuck.

Although each terminal doughnut is 2,300 feet in circumference, MCI's "Drive to the Gate" design means only a 75-foot walk from curbside to boarding.

Sure its an international airport. But in 1987, only 599 foreign visitors deplaned at MCI.

QUICK CONTACTS

Medical . . . 243–5212
Police . . . 243–5215
Lost & Found . . . 243–5215
Information . . . 243–5237
Paging . . . Airlines

THE BASICS

Name: Kansas City International Airport
Airport Code: MCI
Location: 18 miles northwest of Kansas City
Mailing Address: PO Box 20047
Kansas City, MO 64195
Phone: (816) 243–5248
Time: Central
Daily Passengers (Rank): 25,879 (48)
Supervising Body: City of Kansas City Aviation
Department

AIRLINES	PHONES	TERMINAL
All phones Area Code 816 unless otherwise specified.		
Air Midwest	1-800-272-6433	A
America West	1-800-247-5692	A
American	221-7767	A
Braniff	1-800-272-6433	B
Capitol	1-800-272-6433	B
Continental	471-3000	C
Delta	471-1828	B
Eastern	1-800-327-8376	A
Midcontinent	1-800-272-6433	B
Midway	1-800-621-5700	C
Northwest	474-1104	C
Piedmont	1-800-251-5720	C
Southwest	474-1221	B
TWA	842-4000	B
United	471-6060	C
USAir	1-800-428-4322	C

FINDING YOUR WAY AROUND

Three circular terminals, each 2100 feet long and 65
feet wide, are arranged like a shamrock around a
long-term parking area. Terminal A contains Gates 1–
20; Terminal B, Gates 26–40; and Terminal C, Gates
50–66. Each terminal is self-contained and has its own
short-term parking area. Continuously running buses
provide transportation between the terminals.

INFORMATION FOR THE HANDICAPPED

MCI conforms to Architectural and Transportation
Barriers Compliance Board standards. All air travelers
are advised to make advance arrangements with their
carriers if they require special needs. TDD phones are
located near Gates 7, 35, and 58. MCI publishes a
brochure outlining facilities for handicapped and
elderly travelers. For information on ground
transportation for the disabled, call 243–5950.

GROUND TRANSPORTATION

Transportation display boards are located near the
main exits of each terminal.
The Red Bus provides free inter-terminal connections
and also serves the long-term parking lots. Look for
the red Inter-Terminal Connection signs outside each
terminal.

Buses

The KCI Express Green buses board at Gate 63,
Terminal C, and provide service throughout the
Metro area and Johnson County. The buses run every
30 minutes, from 5:45 a.m. to 11:30 p.m. Fares start at
$9. Complete information is available at the ticket
counter, Gate 63.

Car Rentals

Car rental agency phones are located at: Terminal A,
Gates 5, 7, and 12; Terminal B, Gates 28, 31, 34, and
39; Terminal C, Gates 52, 58, and 65. On-Airport firms
are:

Avis	243–5760	Hertz	243–5765
Budget	243–5755	National	243–5770
Dollar	243–5600		

Hotel Shuttles

Courtesy phones are located at Terminal A, Gates 2, 6
and 15; Terminal B, Gates 28, 31, 34 and 39; and
Terminal C, Gates 52, 59, 61 and 64.

Taxis/Limos

Taxi service is available at curbside and is provided by
20 different companies. Fares vary between
companies, but a typical fare to downtown is $22.

Parking

MCI can park 9,800 cars in its 9 lots—it also has 6 different daily rate maximums. The cheapest is Satellite S: $.25/hr., $3 daily maximum. Buses provide free transportation to terminals. Short-term rates in the terminal arcs are $.25/1st half-hr., $10/daily maximum. Rates in all lots except S escalate at the rate of $.50/hr. until the daily maximum is reached. Valet service ($5 surcharge) is also available. For parking radio information, tune to 1610 AM or call 243–5656.

TRAVELERS SERVICES

We said MCI was a "no frills" facility. Amenities are basic, but prices are reasonable and most travelers' needs can be met.

Airline Clubs

American's Admiral	Terminal A, Gate 14.
Eastern's Ionosphere	Terminal A, Gate 6.
TWA's Ambassador	Terminal B, Gate 32.

Baggage Storage

Coin lockers are located in each terminal. Rate: $.50/ 24 hrs.

Banks

There is no full-service banking facility at MCI although there are ATMs in each terminal. A Universal Money Machine is located in Terminal A, Gate 4, and in Terminal C, Gate 58.

Business Services

There are no business services at MCI.

Cocktail Lounges

Six lounges are located at Gates 5, 14, 29, 36, 53, and 62.

Gift Shops/Newsstands

Newsstands and shops serving basic traveler's needs are located at Gates 5, 14, 29, 36, 53, 62.

Hotel

The Marriott Hotel is on-site. Weekday rates start at $109; weekend rates start at $59.

Information

Available by phone only. Phones located at Terminal A, Gates 2, 6, and 15; Terminal B, Gates 28, 31, 34 and 39; Terminal C, Gates 52, 59, 61 and 64.

Military Services

There are no separate facilities for military personnel.

Miscellaneous Services

Barber/Beauty Shops are in each terminal. Open daily, 8 a.m. to 7 p.m. A regular cut is $12.
Nursery: Unattended facilities are located at Gates 8, 33 and 57.
Video game rooms are in each terminal.

Post

Mail drops are in each terminal. Stamps are available from gift shops/newsstands.

Restaurants/Snack Bars

Host Restaurants are at Gates 5, 29 and 52. Snack bars are located at Gates 5, 14, 29, 36, 53 and 62.

TIME TO KILL

MCI's location makes it difficult to get to anything in a reasonable amount of time. So if you have a layover of less than three hours stay put. Round trip to downtown Kansas City by Airport Express is about 90 minutes, which leaves little time to get a feel for this city. If you have four or more hours, we recommend the Crown Center. Hallmark, the greeting card company and Kansas City's largest employer, financed this $500 million, 89-shop, up-to-date plaza. A visitors center, open 9 a.m. to 5 p.m. tells the story of Hallmark, and is free.

For additional information call the Convention and Visitors Bureau 221–5242 or 1–800–523–5953.

LAS VEGAS

McCARRAN INTERNATIONAL AIRPORT

In April 1926, Western Air made the first scheduled flight from a small airstrip located on the corner of Sahara Avenue and Paradise Road. Over 40 years later and no longer located on the "Strip," McCarran International has skyrocketed into a multimillion dollar complex covering 2,000 acres and serving over 585 flights a day. McCarran has come a long way from what was once referred to as the "white elephant basking in the desert sun."

Today, McCarran International Airport ranks 30th world-wide passenger volume and employs over 1,600 people. A simple, clean and very friendly airport, it is undergoing some major changes under the billing of "McCarran 2000." An impressive 20 year expansion project to the tune of $1 billion is planned.

In 1943, a young aviator by the name of George Crockett leased a piece of desert land and built on the airfield which McCarran International sits. George is the great, great, great grandson of another pioneer, Davy Crockett.

In the early days, concession stands were minimal but Las Vegas Airport had space for 9 slot machines. The "take" was greater on the machines than on the airline tickets.

Over 90% of deplaning passengers are either conventioners or tourists. No need to bring an umbrella here. Las Vegas boasts bountiful sunshine—an average of 315 days a year, and median temperatures in the high 70s.

In 1982, McCarran's expansion was the subject of the largest airport bond sale in history, generating over $300 million.

QUICK CONTACTS

Medical. . . . First Aid—739–5620, 8:30 a.m. to 5 p.m.
               Operations Center—739–5201, 24 hours
Police. . . . 739–5201
Lost & Found. . . . 739–5134 (all articles except baggage) M–F, 8 a.m. to 5 p.m.
739–5630 (after hours and holidays)
Information. . . . 739–5434 (8 a.m.) to 5 p.m. or 798–5410 (24 hr. recording)
Paging. . . . 739–5733

THE BASICS

Name: McCarran International Airport
Airport Code: LAS
Location: 6 miles south of Las Vegas
Mailing Address: PO Box 11005
                 Airport Station
                 Las Vegas, NV 89111
Telephone: (702) 739–5211
Time: Pacific
Daily Passenger (Rank): 40,123 (30)
Supervising Body: Board of County Commissioners
                  Clark County, NV

AIRLINE	TELEPHONE	GATES
Air America	800–247–2475	C
Air Canada	800–422–6232	C
Air Nevada	736–8900	R
America West	386–0791	B
American	385–3781	C
Braniff	800–272–6433	B
Continental	800–525–0280	B
Delta	385–3000	A
Eastern	385–1160	A
Golden Pacific	528–7146	
Havasu	800–528–8047	R
Hawaiian Air	736–0088	B
Midway Airlines	800–621–5700	C

AIRLINE	TELEPHONE	GATES
Northwest	800–225–2525	A
Scenic Airline	739–1900	Regional
Skywest	800–453–9415	A
Southwest	382–1221	C
Sunworld Airways	736–4111	B
TWA	385–1000	C
United	385–3222	C
USAir	382–1905	A

FINDING YOUR WAY AROUND

McCarran International consists of one central terminal with a connecting satellite concourse (via a people mover) and two main concourses on the western end of the complex (via moving walkways). In the central terminal on the second level (esplanade) you will find concessions, restaurants and other amenities. The International Terminal is located on the northern end of the terminal complex.

INFORMATION FOR THE HANDICAPPED

McCarran International provides facilities for the handicapped and elderly that are in accordance with the standards of the Architectural and Transportation Barriers Compliance Board. All airports emphasize notifying the airline you are traveling with ahead of time if you need special assistance. McCarran Airport also produces a guide with information for the handicapped or elderly titled, "A Special Guide To McCarran International Airport." Write to the airport or call (702) 739–5211. TDD's are located at the four public information booths (3 in the Central Terminal, 1 at the west end of Gate C), the Travelers Aid booth and the police substation.

GROUND TRANSPORTATION

The ground transportation services are located on the ground level. A bus plaza has been set aside for tour buses at the southern end of the ticketing area (Central Terminal). Taxi fare is $13–$15 and is the least expensive way to travel downtown.
Hotel courtesy phones are located in the baggage claim area.

Buses

No public bus transportation.
Charter Buses: Gray Line 739–5489
Ray & Ross Transport Inc. 646–4661
Westside Charter Service Inc. 385–5949
Las Vegas/Tonopah/Reno Stage Lines 384–1230

Car Rentals

Car rental counters are located in the center baggage claim area.

All State	736–6147	Hertz	736–4900
Avis	739–5595	National	739–5395
Dollar	739–8400	Sav-Mor	736–1234

Taxis/Limos

A taxi stand is located outside the baggage claim area (west side). Fare to downtown: $13–$15.
Three limousine companies are located in the center of the baggage claim area.

Gray Line	739–5489
Lucky 7	739–6177
Bell Trans	739–7990

Parking

Fifteen minute parking at the baggage claim/arrivals curb is available but the departure curb is for drop-off only. For additional information, call 739–5469.
Covered Parking: 15 minutes free. $.25/ea. addit. 15 min., $6/day.
Uncovered Parking: $.25/every 15 min., $4/day.

TRAVELERS SERVICES

The amenities at Las Vegas Airport are excellent. Mutual of Omaha's Passenger Service Center provides extensive business services, and there is an abundance of interesting stores to browse in and tempting restaurants and concessions to please the palette. And while you are wandering, take a good look around you. This is a very attractive airport. It has clean, bold, contemporary architecture with an interior that echoes the style and flair of some of the finest hotels on the "Strip."

Airline Clubs

None

Baggage Storage

Mutual of Omaha's Passenger Service Center (center of ticketing) offers storage for luggage, skis and other items. Phone: 739–5650.

Rates: carry-on—$1.50/1 to 24 hrs.
    standard—$2.50/1 to 24 hrs.
    oversized—$3.50/1 to 24 hrs.
    miscellaneous—$3.50/1 to 24 hrs.

Open from 6:30 a.m. to 9:30 p.m. and no length of stay limit.

Lockers: Located in the concourse area of Gates A, B and C. $.75/first day, $1/each additional day.

Banks

First Interstate Bank: 2nd floor (Esplanade)
10 a.m. to 4 p.m. M–Th, 10 a.m. to 5:40 p.m. F.
Foreign Money Exchange: Mutual of Omaha's (PSC)
6:30 a.m. to 9:30 p.m.
ATMs: Waiting Area Bridge

Business Services

Mutual of Omaha's Passenger Service Center offers secretarial services, notary, photocopying, faxing, communication services, foreign currency exchange, Western Union, and shower facilities. Located in the passenger ticketing level. Hours: 6:30 a.m. to 9:30 p.m. Call 739–5650

Cocktail Lounges

Main Terminal area and concourses.

Gift Shops/Newsstands

The shopping at LAS offers an interesting selection. For the numismatist/philatelist—The Coin Shop, for the bibliophile or wine aficionado—The Book and Wine Shop, for the botanist—Forget Me Not Inc. and for the romantic—French Room Lingerie. All are located in the Main Terminal Building.

Hotel

No on-site hotel.

Information/Assistance

Four information booths: (1 in the south end of the terminal complex, 3 in Esplanade East at level 2). They are staffed from 7 a.m. to 10 p.m., 7 days a week. Call 739–5094.

Travelers Aid Booth: Located between the baggage claim areas at level 1. Open 7 days a week, 8 a.m. to 5 p.m. Call 739–5234

Military Services

None

Miscellaneous

Chapel: None on the airport but Las Vegas has more churches per capita than any other city in the world. Over 59,000 are married each year in either a church or chapel. Talk about gambling.

Shower facilities: Mutual of Omaha's Passenger Service Center (Main Terminal). For $7.50 you can sing and shower away that tired feeling. The price includes all sorts of goodies: soap, towel, shampoo, hair dryer, deodorant and electric shaver. Open daily from 6:30 a.m. to 9:30 p.m. Call 739–5650

Post

A post office is located in the Passenger Service Center (Main Terminal).

Restaurants/Snack Bars

The Main Terminal houses a full-service restaurant called Esplanade. It is open from 6 a.m. to 8 p.m. and offers American-style food. Also in the Main Terminal is a Food Express with a little-bit-of-this and a little-bit-of-that: pizza and pasta, oriental, hamburgers and chicken, pastries, and soft yogurt to mention a few. There are delectables for the sweet tooth, Ethel M. Chocolates serving homemade candy and Creative Candy and Gifts offers its fudge and other captivating confections.

TIME TO KILL

1 hour. . . . As mentioned earlier, LAS is an attractive airport. Take a walk. And just for the fun of it, ride the moving walkway. Any number of celebrities, like

Bob Hope, Kenny Rogers, or Teresa Brewer will sing to you. Or let the comedic humor of Rodney Dangerfield and Rich Little tickle your funny bone while carefully reminding you of certain safety precautions—recorded messages from the stars.

Or. . . . Visit the Freedom Shrine and peruse through some of our Nation's historical documents. Located near security, toward C Gates.

2 hours. . . . Tours of the McCarran Airport are available, Monday through Friday, Saturday upon request. Check with the information counter.

Or. . . . Trek over to the parking garage and from the 6th floor you can capture a beautiful view of Las Vegas.

3 hours. . . . This reminder is probably unnecessary but you could try your hand at Lady Luck. Hail a cab and hit the closest hotel. Or if you don't feel like riding into town, try the airport slot machines; they're everywhere.

Or. . . . The Liberace Museum is a safe bet. Open daily from 10 a.m. to 5 p.m. Admission: $6.50/adults, $4.50/seniors and $2.00 for children. Call 731–1775

4 hours or more. . . . If time and budget permits, see a show. If your schedule does not allow for a show take a cab into Las Vegas the "city that never sleeps."

For the more adventurous . . . Scenic Airlines, based a few minutes from McCarran, offers an exciting 1 hour flight over Hoover Dam and the western rim of the Grand Canyon. They call it the Western Rim tour. It costs around $73. Flights depart at 8 a.m. and 3 p.m. daily.

And for a bigger thrill . . . you can take the deluxe tour of the Grand Canyon. Winging your way over to the south rim will take 3 hours and a great deal of courage. It is spectacular and worth it. Cost: $126. Flights depart at 7 a.m., 8 a.m., 10:45 a.m., 2:30 p.m. and 3:30 p.m. Call (702) 739–1900

For additional information call the Las Vegas Convention and Visitors Authority. (702) 733–2323

LOS ANGELES

LOS ANGELES
INTERNATIONAL AIRPORT

The newest addition to LAX is the 5-story Tom Bradley International Terminal, but the real showstopper is the Theme Building. Right out of Buck Rogers and the twenty-first century, it is the focal point of this modern and exciting airport. Located in the center of the terminal complex, its arches extend skyward to 135 feet with a dramatic observation tower at the pinnacle.

Because the frequent business traveler makes up half of all the airline traffic in this airport, LAX has done its best to focus on the needs of the executive. Its 3 business centers are the most comprehensive of any airport and offer everything from conference rooms to the use of personal computers.

LAX also caters to the overseas passenger. After an international flight, weary and worn, you can shower and relax in one of the 13 mini-hotel rooms at LAX.

Individuals of the following nationalities have owned the land on which LAX is built: Mexican (1837), Scottish (1860), Canadian (1885), and finally a native of Los Angeles in 1894.

The Tom Bradley International Terminal has a departure area the size of 3 football fields, which comes in handy considering that almost 123,000 passengers pass through here a day. It also houses the nation's largest airport restaurant—with 27,000 square feet and seating for more than 700 people.

QUICK CONTACTS
Medical. . . . 215–6000
Police. . . . 646–4268

Lost & Found. . . . 417–0440
Information. . . . 646–5252
Paging. . . . Airlines

THE BASICS

Name: Los Angeles International Airport
Airport Code: LAX
Location: 12 miles southwest of downtown Los
        Angeles
Mailing Address: One World Way
Los Angeles, CA 90009
Telephone: (213) 646–5252
Time: Pacific
Daily Passenger Rank: 122,940 (3)
Supervising Body: Department of Airports
                City of Los Angeles

AIRLINE	TELEPHONE	TERMINAL
Aerolineas Argentinas	1–800–333–0276	Intl
Aeromexico	1–800–237–6679	Intl
Air America	1–800–247–2475	7
Air Canada	1–800–422–6232	2
Air France	1–800–237–2747	Intl
Air Jamaica	1–800–523–5585	Intl
Air LA	641–1114	It
Air New Zealand	1–800–262–1234	Intl
Alaska Airlines	1–800–682–2221	4
Alitalia	568–0901	It
Alpha	417–9744	It
America West	746–6400	1
American Airlines	935–6045	4
American Eagle	935–6045	4
American Transair	1–800–225–2995	Intl
ANA	646–1480	Intl
Avianca	1–800–284–2622	2
Balair	646–0089	Intl
Braniff	1–800–272–6433	1
British Airways	1–800–247–9297	Intl
British Airtours	1–800–826–6547	Intl

AIRLINE	TELEPHONE	TERMINAL
CAAC	384–2703	2
Canadian Airlines International	1–800–426–7000	Intl
China Airlines	1–800–227–5118	Int
Condor	646–4900	Intl
Continental	772–6000	6
Delta	386–5510	5
Eastern	772–5800	6
Ecuatoriana	627–0615	Intl
El Al	1–800–223–6700	Intl
Finnair	646–1948	Intl
Garunda	1–800–332–2223	Intl
Hawaiian	1–800–367–5320	2
Iberia	1–800–221–9741	Intl
Japan Airlines	620–9580	Intl
KLM	1–800–777–5553	Intl
Korean	484–1900	Intl
LACSA	383–5140	Intl
LA Helicopter	642–6600	P-4
Lan Chile	1–800–225–5526	Intl
LOT	1–800–223–0593	Intl
LTU	640–1940	Intl
Lufthansa	1–800–645–3880	Intl
MGM Grand Air	568–4100	It
Malaysian	642–0849	Intl
Martinair	1–800–521–6565	7
Mexicana	687–8320	Intl
Nippon	646–1116	
Northwest	1–800–225–2525	2
Pan Am	1–800–221–1111	2
Pan Am Bridge	1–800–221–1111	2
Philippine Airlines	1–800–135–9725	Intl
Piedmont	977–4937	1
Qantas	1–800–227–4500	Intl
Resorts	1–800–999–9163	2
Royal Jordanian	215–1736	Intl
SAS	655–8600	Intl
Singapore	655–9270	Intl
Sky West	386–5510	6
Skyworld	646–0089	2
Southwest	485–1211	1
StatesWest	1–800–247–3866	3L
Sun Country	646–0089	1
TACA	629–1159	Intl
TWA	484–2244	3

AIRLINE	TELEPHONE	TERMINAL
United	772–2121	7
United Express	772–2121	7
USAir	935–5005	1
UTA	1–800–282–4484	Intl
Varig	1–800–468–2744	Intl
Wardair	1–800–237–0314	6
Yugoslav	338–0379	Intl

(Intl = Bradley International Terminal, It = Imperial Terminal)

FINDING YOUR WAY AROUND

Los Angeles Airport is arranged in a U-shape with eight individual terminals; 1 to 7 and the Tom Bradley International Terminal. Projecting from each terminal is a satellite building for airline gates.

Located at the south side of the airfield is the Imperial Terminal, designed for supplementing carriers. There is a two-level roadway system—the lower level is for passenger arrivals and the upper level is for departures.

LAX is well equipped to handle the foreign traveler. Most of the international arrivals and departures are in the Tom Bradley International Terminal. Two Visitor Centers with multilingual assistance are located at the Tom Bradley International Terminal and a "Welcome" brochure which contains airport information in several different languages is available at the Visitors Center.

INFORMATION FOR THE HANDICAPPED

Los Angeles Airport provides facilities for the handicapped and elderly in accordance with the requirements set by the Architectural and Transportation Barriers Compliance Board. For the brochure, "Guide for the Handicapped and Elderly," write or call the airport.

TDD's are located in Terminals 2, 3, 6, and 7, in the Tom Bradley International Terminal (arrivals level) and in the Terminal 1 concourse. For additional information call (213) 417–0439 or 1–800–342–5833.

LOS ANGELES INTERNATIONAL AIRPORT

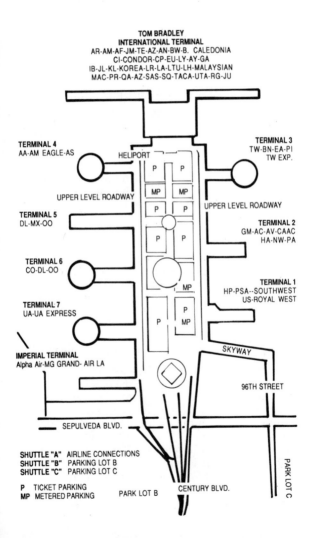

**TOM BRADLEY
INTERNATIONAL TERMINAL**
AR-AM-AF-JM-TE-AZ-AN-BW-B. CALEDONIA
CI-CONDOR-CP-EU-LY-AY-GA
IB-JL-KL-KOREA-LR-LA-LTU-LH-MALAYSIAN
MAC-PR-QA-AZ-SAS-SQ-TACA-UTA-RG-JU

TERMINAL 4
AA-AM EAGLE-AS

HELIPORT

TERMINAL 3
TW-BN-EA-PI
TW EXP.

UPPER LEVEL ROADWAY

UPPER LEVEL ROADWAY

TERMINAL 5
DL-MX-OO

TERMINAL 2
GM-AC-AV-CAAC
HA-NW-PA

TERMINAL 6
CO-DL-OO

TERMINAL 1
HP-PSA--SOUTHWEST
US-ROYAL WEST

TERMINAL 7
UA-UA EXPRESS

IMPERIAL TERMINAL
Alpha Air-MG GRAND- AIR LA

SKYWAY

96TH STREET

SEPULVEDA BLVD.

SHUTTLE "A" AIRLINE CONNECTIONS
SHUTTLE "B" PARKING LOT B
SHUTTLE "C" PARKING LOT C

P TICKET PARKING
MP METERED PARKING

PARK LOT B

CENTURY BLVD.

PARK LOT C

P

MP

LOS ANGELES

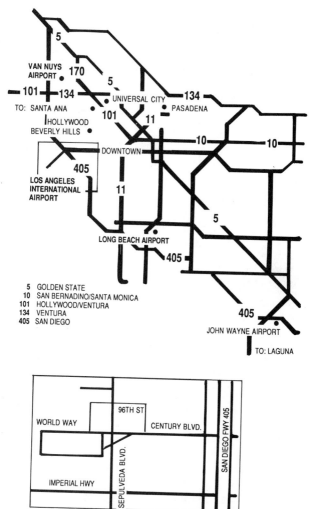

5 GOLDEN STATE
10 SAN BERNARDINO/SANTA MONICA
101 HOLLYWOOD/VENTURA
134 VENTURA
405 SAN DIEGO

GROUND TRANSPORTATION

On the lower level of each terminal are signs denoting
a particular form of transport; Taxi, Van Stop, Bus
Stop, Courtesy Tram, and LAX Shuttle. An
information board with a direct telephone line is in
each baggage claim area. A ground transportation
information booth is located outside the baggage
claim area of each terminal and is staffed from 8 a.m.
to midnight daily. Tickets are sold by individual
ground transportation operators.

Airport Shuttles

"LAX SHUTTLE" Free transport between terminals
and parking lots. All shuttles are white with blue and
green stripes. There are four types: "A" Airline
Connections, "B" Airport Parking (Lot B), "C" Airport
Parking (Lot C) and "I" Imperial Terminal.

Buses

City Buses: "LAX Shuttle" (Airport Parking, lot C).
City bus service operates from Lot C (96th St.).
Scheduled Buses: "Bus Stop" Information and tickets
are available at sidewalk booths in front of the
terminals.
Door-to Door Buses: "Van Stop" Information and
tickets are available in front of the terminals.

Car Rentals

Car rental counters are located at each terminal arrival
level in the central terminal area.

Avis	646–5600	Hertz	646–4861
Budget	645–4500	National	670–4950
Dollar	645–9333		

Hotel Shuttles

Located in the baggage claim areas are hotel/bus
information boards and courtesy phones to arrange
for accomodations. Shuttles depart to hotels from the
"Tram Stop" sign.

Taxis/Limos

Taxis: Located curbside at the lower level of the
terminals. The fare from the airport to downtown is

$6.50 and takes approximately 45 minutes. The "Taxi" sign is the pickup point.

Limos: Board at the curb outside the terminals. For information use the hotel/bus board and courtesy phones in the baggage claim areas.

Parking

Parking is either in the central terminal complex area or on the fringe. Central parking is the most expensive and preferred for short-term while long-term parking with free shuttle service is readily available. For additional information call (213) 646–2911.

Central Terminal Parking: Lots (1 to 7)
$1/ea. hr., $10/ea. 24 hrs.
Lots C and D: First 2 hours free,
$.50/ea. additional 2 hrs., $4/24 hrs.
Lot B: First 2 hours free,
$.50/ea. additional 2 hrs., $3/24 hrs.
Imperial Terminal: $.50/2 hrs., $5/24 hrs.
Parking information: (818) AIRPORT or radio AM 530.

TRAVELERS SERVICES

Like L.A.'s smog, amenities for the traveler blanket this airport. It has the largest airport restaurant, a 13 room mini-hotel, 3 business centers, and numerous gift shops and concessions.

Airline Clubs

All clubs are on the mezzanine level unless otherwise indicated.

Air Canada's Maple Leaf	Terminal 2
American's Admiral Club	Terminal 4
Continental's Presidents Club	Terminal 6
Delta's Crown Room	Terminal 5 (3rd level).
Eastern's Ionosphere	Terminal 6
Northwest Orient's World Club	Terminal 2
Pan Am's Clipper Club	Terminal 2
TWA's Ambassadors Club	Terminal 3
United's Red Carpet Room	Terminal 7 (Near gates 70A & 70B).

| United's Royal Pacific Room 1st Class (International Passengers only) | Terminal 7 |
| USAir | Terminal 1 |

Baggage Storage

Baggage storage: Business Centers in Terminals 1, 4 and 7.
6 a.m. to 10:30 p.m. Price: (24 hrs.)
$1.50/carry-on, $2.25/medium, $3.50/large.
ABC storage in the International Terminal.
6 a.m. to 11:30 p.m. Call 646–7889
Lockers: All terminals, $.75 to $1 for first 24 hours, $2 each additional 24 hour period.

Banks

There are no full service banks.
Bank of America: Tom Bradley International Terminal
Citicorp and Bank of America: Terminals 1, 4, and 7.
Currency Exchange: Terminals 2, 5, and International.
Other money exchange is located at insurance counters in other terminals.
ATMs: Tom Bradley International Terminal and Terminals 2, 3, 4, 5, 6, and 7.

Business Services

Mutual of Omaha's Business Service Centers are located in Terminals 1, 4, and 7. Hours: 6 am to 10:30 p.m.
The following services are available:
Foreign currency exchange
Pagers
Photocopiers and electronic mail
Private conference rooms
Reduced rate on long distance telephone service
Secretarial services
Telex and telegram service
Word processing and personal computers
For additional information call
Terminal 1, 646–4934
Terminal 4, 646–2929
Terminal 7, 646–7934

Cocktail Lounges

Cocktail lounges are located in all the terminals.

Gift Shops/Newsstands

The duty free shops are the only stores to get excited about and unless you are traveling overseas you are not permitted to purchase items here. Duty Free Shops: Terminals 2, 3, 4, 5, and the Tom Bradley International Terminal. Additional airport gift shops and newsstands are located in all terminals.

Hotels

Skytel: Mini-Hotel service. Located in the Tom Bradley International Terminal (upper level). Rent a room by the hour. $16/1st hr., $32/4 hrs., $47/8 hrs. Just want to shower? $7.95/½ hr.
We recommend you call ahead for reservation, (213) 417–0200.

Information/Assistance

In the Tom Bradley International Terminal there are two visitor centers which provide multilingual assistance and information for passengers needing additional help. Open 8 a.m. to 11:30 p.m. No information counters are in the other terminals. Contact airline personnel or Traveler's Aid for information. Traveler's Aid is located in all the terminals. This service provides direction and assistance to all travelers. Call 646–2270.

Military Services

USO: Terminal 4. Hours: daily, 11 a.m. to 5 p.m. It is open longer when military flights arrive.

Miscellaneous

Christian Science Reading Room: Terminal 7. Hours: 8 a.m. to 6 p.m.
First Aid Station: Located in the Tom Bradley International Terminal. Open daily. 7 a.m. to 11 p.m. Call 215–6000.

Post

Stamp vending machines and mail drops are located in all the terminals.

Restaurants/Snack Bars

California Place tops the list. It is a full service
restaurant at the pinnacle of the Theme Building. Not
only does it offer excellent dining (fresh seafood is the
specialty), but a panoramic view of Los Angeles as
well. Don't choke, but the dinners start at $18.00.
Non-smokers are seated with a view of Beverly Hills
while smokers can gape at El Segundo. It is open M–
Sat. Lunch is served from 11 a.m. to 2:30 p.m. Dinner
is served from 5 p.m. to 10 p.m. Reservations are
highly recommended. Call 645–5471.
There are cafeterias and snack bars in all the
terminals.

TIME TO KILL

1 hour. . . . If you are not hungry or don't want to
cough up the money for a meal at the California
Place, the observation deck at the Theme Building is
worth the visit. On a clear day, you can see Los
Angeles. Open 9 a.m. to 5 p.m.

2 hours. . . . L.A. County Art Museum. Open 10 a.m.
to 5 p.m. T—Sun. Admission is $4. (213) 624–7300.

3 hours. . . . Place your bets. Fifteen minutes by cab
and you'll be at the Hollywood Park. The season runs
from April to July and from November to December.
Post time: 1 p.m. Grandstand seats are $2.75. Call
(213) 419–1500 for more information.

4 hours or more. . . . The Forum. This is where the
Lakers perform for Jack Nicholson and Jack Nicholson
performs for the Lakers. And in this wonderland of
sports the Great Gretsky chases a hockey puck at
almost $2,000 a minute. But if basketball and hockey
is not your cup of tea, they also have tennis, soccer,
boxing and an occasional concert. For information call
(213) 673–1300.

For additional information call the Greater Los
Angeles Visitors and Convention Bureau, (213) 624–
7300 or (213) 689–8822.

MEMPHIS

MEMPHIS INTERNATIONAL AIRPORT

Memphis International is called "Mid-America's Gateway to the World." Just 50 miles south of the exact population center of the U. S., MEM's location makes it a natural center for national and multi-regional distribution. Originally a 202-acre site with a sod runway and accomodating 15 passengers a day, MEM has grown to 3,600 acres and now has over 20 miles of runways and taxiways.

MEM was designated by the FAA as a "Large Hub" in 1986. That status was conferred when MEM passed the one per cent mark as a handler of air passengers.

MEM is home to Federal Express. The overnight package carrier averages 127 operations a day.

QUICK CONTACTS

Medical . . . 458–3311
Police . . . 922–8298
Lost & Found . . . 922–8298
Information . . . 922–8000
Paging . . . Airlines

THE BASICS

Name: Memphis International Airport
Airport Code: MEM
Location: 9 miles southeast of Memphis
Telephone: (901) 922–8000
Mailing Address: PO Box 30168
                 Memphis, TN 38130

Time: Central
Daily Passengers (Rank): 29,632 (36)
Supervising Body: Memphis-Shelby County Airport
Authority

AIRLINES	TELEPHONE	TERMINAL
American	526–8861	C
Delta	922–8241	A
Midway	922–8353	C
Northwest	922–8451	B
Northwest Airlink	922–8580	B
Piedmont	526–0661	C
TWA	922–8150	C
United	922–8688	C
USAir	922–8261	C

FINDING YOUR WAY AROUND

MEM has three terminals (A, B, C) with B considered
the main terminal. Each terminal has a concourse and
gates are numbered respectively. International arrivals
are at gate C-3.

INFORMATION FOR THE HANDICAPPED

MEM provides facilities for handicapped and elderly
travelers in accordance with Architectural and
Transportation Compliance Board standards. All
passengers requiring special assistance are advised to
consult with their airline carriers prior to departure. A
TDD unit is located in the police office in Terminal A,
ground level.

GROUND TRANSPORTATION

All ground transportation departs from the ground
level in front of the three terminals. There is no public
bus transportation.

Car Rentals

Direct connection phones are located in the baggage
claims area of each terminal. Free shuttle vans
provide transportation to the car rental pick-up sites.

Taxis/Limos

All cabs are metered. Minimum fare is $5. Fare to downtown is $12.
Van service is also available. Fare to downtown locations is $6.

Parking

Short term rates: $1/first hr., $12/daily max.
Long term: $1/ first hr., $6/daily max.
Reduced rate: $1/first hr, $4/daily max.
For parking information call 922–8088. Radio broadcast 1610 AM also provides parking information.

TRAVELERS SERVICES

Services are ample and surprisingly varied. Not many airports have a Polynesian restaurant, but MEM does. Several fine shops, a gourmet chocolate shop, and lounges with motifs ranging from modernistic pink neon to rustic WW I can be found.

Airline Clubs

Delta's Crown Room   Terminal A.
Northwest's World Club   Concourse B.

Baggage Storage

Coin lockers are on all concourses. Rates start at $.25/ 24 hrs. for small cases.
Storage is also available at Tele-Trip in the Terminal B lobby.

Banks

Tele-Trip Currency Exchange. Hours daily are 7 a.m. to 9 p.m. Call 922–8090.
Automatic Teller Machines are located in the Terminal B lobby.
There is no full-service bank.

Business Services

Tele-Trip Travelers Services is located in the Terminal B lobby for copying, faxing, and notary. Hours: daily, 7 a.m. to 9 p.m.

Cocktail Lounges

Waldo Pepper is a lounge decorated in a World War I
motif. It is located in Concourse B. Open M—Sat.
from 8 a.m. to 9 p.m., on Sundays from noon to
6 p.m. The Veranda is a pink neon and mahogany
lounge located in Terminal C.

Gift Shops/Newsstands

Five gift shops and newsstands are scattered
throughout the airport. Maxine's sells fine gifts. For
something really different try the Sweet on Memphis
chocolate shop in Concourse C. Open daily, 8 a.m.–
8:30 p.m. Take home a King of Rock and Roll, an
8-ounce chocolate sculpture for $7.50.

Hotel

Skyport Hotel is located in the lobby of Terminal A.
Rates start at $39. Call 345–3220.

Information/Assistance

The Tele-Trip booth in the Terminal B ticket lobby
functions as an information reference point.

Military Assistance

A military assistance booth is located in Terminal A.
Hours: 8:30 a.m. to 11:30 p.m., daily. Call 398–3661.

Miscellaneous

Barber/beauty shop: Located on the second level
between Terminals B and C.
Game Room: Located on the second level between
Terminals B and C. Open 24 hours.
Nursery changing room: Located on the west end of
Terminal B ticket lobby.
The Airport Travel Center: Located on the second
level next to Terminal A. Call 398–3900.

Post

Mail drops and stamp vending machines are located
throughout the complex.

Restaurants/Snack Bars

There are 22 dining establishments throughout MEM,
ranging from the casual snackbar to the near elegant.

The Luau Polynesian is located on the mezzanine
level of Terminal B. Open daily from 11 a.m.–9 p.m.
Sweetwaters is a fresh seafood/raw bar establishment.

TIME TO KILL

1 hour . . . The Aviation Historical Room in the
Terminal B ticket lobby is free and open 24 hours a
day. On display are photos, memorabilia, and models
highlighting Memphis aviation.

2 hours . . . You promised yourself you would never
do anything like this, but go ahead. A $5 taxi fare and
five minutes will bring you to Graceland. Open daily
9 a.m. to 5 p.m., you can tour the grounds, trophy
room, and Meditation Gardens (where Elvis is
buried). The tour takes about 90 minutes. Call ahead
(332–3322) because this is one hot spot. Admission is
$7.50.

3 hours . . . The Duck Walk. Everyday at 11 a.m. (you
can set your watch) five ducks exit their $15,000
penthouse atop the historic Peabody Hotel and walk
across the street to the tunes of a Sousa march and
swim in the pond. At 5 p.m. they return with the
same pomp and circumstance. The airport van will
get you there for $6. You're also in the vicinity of
Beale Street so even if you miss the little quackers you
can pound the pavement of this legendary birth-of-
the-blues thoroughfare.

4 hours . . . The Pink Palace started out as the
exclusive showcase residence of Clarence Saunders,
founder of Piggly Wiggly—forerunner to today's
supermarkets. Saunders lost his money in the Stock
Market Crash and Memphis ended up with an
impressive social and natural history museum. Hours
vary depending on the time of year. Admission is $3.
Call 454–5600.

For additional information call the Memphis Visitors
Center, (901) 526–4880.

MIAMI

MIAMI INTERNATIONAL AIRPORT

Miami International Airport has a long and storied history in the development of U.S. air travel. Carved by Pan Am in 1928 out of palmetto scrub lands once owned by the Seminole Fruit and Land Company, MIA was the third U.S.-designated airport of entry. Eastern Airlines was born here; the nation's first scheduled jet passenger plane landed here in 1958. From 2,000-foot runways on a site bisected by railroad tracks, MIA has become the nation's second largest international passenger volume terminal (behind JFK), deplaning 4.4 million foreign visitors each year. In 1936, Eastern trumpeted 52 passengers a day; MIA now handles 52 passengers every 16 seconds. Will Rogers called Miami the "jumping off place of the world," and a few hours observing the traveling throngs will leave you believing MIA is the springboard.

In the 1930's, a Newark to Miami flight took 13 hours and cost $74—one-way. Today that same trip takes 2-and-a-half hours but costs 2-and-a-half times more.

When Pan Am built its terminal on the MIA site in 1929 the facility was the first passenger complex as we know airports today. The old terminal was demolished to make way for the present facilities in the early 1960s.

If you're heading for the Islands and you left Keokuk without proof of citizenship, the ground level baggage check rooms will "document" you for $3.

Quick Contacts

Medical . . . 871–7070
Police . . . 871–7373
Lost & Found . . . 871–7377
Information . . . 871–7000
Paging . . . 871–7000

The Basics

Name: Miami International Airport
Airport Code: MIA
Location: 5 miles west of downtown Miami
Mailing Address: PO Box 592075 AMF
                 Miami, FL 33159
Telephone: (305) 871–7000
Time: Eastern
Daily Passengers (Rank): 63,853 (11)
Supervising Body: Metro-Dade County Aviation
                 Authority

AIRLINE	TELEPHONE	CONCOURSE
Aero Coach	1–800–432–5034	F
Aero Peru	526–5744	E
Aerolineas Argentina	371–4800	E
Air Canada	1–800–422–6232	F
Air France	526–6210	E
Air Haiti	871–5890	D
Air Jamaica	358–1121	D
Air Panama	593–1131	E
Airways Int'l	526–3852	F
ALM	871–5340	E
American	358–6800	G
Avensa	871–6605	E
Avianca	526–3371	E
Aviateca	526–6401	E
Bahamas Air	593–1910	G
Balair	871–2458	D
Braniff	1–800–272–6433	D
British Airways	526–5260	D
BWIA	371–2942	E
Cayman	446–8696	E
Continental	371–8421	D
Delta	448–7000	H
Dominicana	526–6942	D

AIRLINE	TELEPHONE	CONCOURSE
Eastern	873–3000	D,E
Ecuatoriana	592–0200	E
El Al	1–800–223–6700	E
Faucett	591–0610	E
Guyana	871–1691	D
Iberia	526–6698	E
LAB	374–4600	E
LACSA	593–0967	E
Ladeco	371–2799	D
Lan Chile	591–3700	E
LAP	533–0337	E
LTU	861–2113	E
Lufthansa	526–6520	E
Mexicana	526–6214	D
Midway	1–800–621–5700	D
Northwest	377–0311	F
Pan Am	874–5000	E,F
Piedmont	358–3396	G
Royal Jordanian	599–0800	E
Surinam	871–3602	E
TACA	358–0066	E
TAN	871–6358	E
TWA	371–7471	G
United	377–3461	G
USAir	1–800–428–4322	G
Varig	358–4935	F
VIASA	374–5000	E
Virgin Air	526–6668	E

Finding Your Way Around

A U-shaped terminal feeds air travelers onto seven
concourses (B-H). Moving sidewalks (called
Skyriders) at the third level connect the parking
garages to the terminal and provide easy transport
between the concourses. The International Terminal is
reached by automated rail cars departing from the
third level of Concourse E. The focal point of all
activity is E. Most of the shops, the hotel, the
information booth, and a number of restaurant/snack
bars are clustered here. MIA is very security
conscious and all concourses are accessible only after
clearing checkpoints. At peak boarding times this

MIAMI INTERNATIONAL AIRPORT

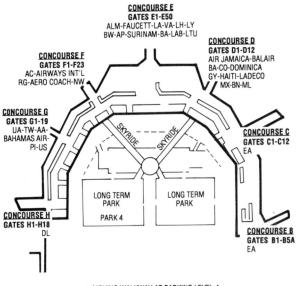

CONCOURSE E
GATES E1-E50
ALM-FAUCETT-LA-VA-LH-LY
BW-AP-SURINAM-BA-LAB-LTU

CONCOURSE D
GATES D1-D12
AIR JAMAICA-BALAIR
BA-CO-DOMINICA
GY-HAITI-LADECO
MX-BN-ML

CONCOURSE F
GATES F1-F23
AC-AIRWAYS INT'L
RG-AERO COACH-NW

CONCOURSE G
GATES G1-19
UA-TW-AA-
BAHAMAS AIR-
PI-US

CONCOURSE C
GATES C1-C12
EA

SKYRIDE SKYRIDE

LONG TERM PARK

LONG TERM PARK

PARK 4

CONCOURSE H
GATES H1-H18
DL

CONCOURSE B
GATES B1-B5A
EA

• • MOVING WALKWAY AT PARKING LEVEL 4
    TO TERMINAL BUILDING.
  • SKYRIDE IS AVAILABLE FROM CONCOURSE B
    THROUGH H

FIRST FLOOR
AGRICULTURE & PUBLIC HEALTH   CAR RENTAL
BAGGAGE CHECK   FOREIGN EXCHANGE
BAGGAGE CLAIM   U.S. CUSTOMS, IMMIGRATION
BUSES, LIMOSINES & TAXIS

MIAMI AREA

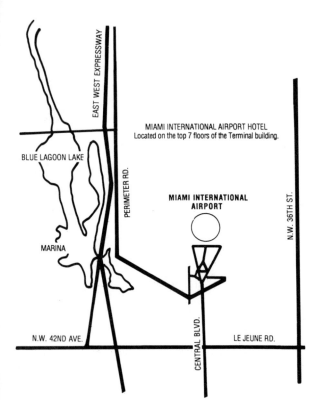

causes bottlenecks that spill passenger lines over into the terminal.

Information for the Handicapped

MIA provides facilities for handicapped and elderly travelers in accordance with Architectural and Transportation Barriers Compliance Board standards. A TDD unit is available around the clock at the information booth at the Concourse E entranceway.

Ground Transportation

Sprawling Dade County is a complicated place to venture. Multi-lingual-staffed Ground Transportation Centers are located throughout the ground floor areas. Always check at these centers about transportation, routes, schedules, and prices. For a hotel shuttle van pickup call direct as there are no courtesy phone banks.

Buses

Metro Dade Transit provides frequent service throughout Dade County. The stop is at the ground level, across from Concourse E. The fare is $1, exact change (no dollar bills).

Car Rentals

Agencies are located on the ground floor of the terminal.

Avis	526–3005	Hertz	871–0300
Budget	871–3053	National	526–5200
Dollar	887–6000	Value	871–6760

Taxis/Limos

A cab starter is located at ground level, near E concourse. Rates: $1.80/1st mile, but there is a minimum charge of $4.50. Fare to downtown Miami is $12.

Red Top Limousine Service has an office at ground level. Minimum charge is $35.

Various firms offer van transport throughout the South Florida area. Rate is $6.75 to downtown Miami, $11.50 to Ft. Lauderdale, $15 to Homestead.

Parking

MIA can park 9,800 vehicles, most of them in covered garages adjacent to the terminal. Short term rates: $2/hr., $18 daily max.; long term garage parking is $2/hr., $6/daily max. For parking information call 871-7536.

Travelers Services

MIA teems with shops and eateries and is constantly adding to the variety of travelers amenities available. Prices are high, but then you didn't fly to Miami to hunt for bargains.

Airline Clubs

Delta's Crown	Concourse H
Eastern's Ionosphere	Concourse B,C
Pan Am's Clipper	Concourse F
Piedmont's Presidential	Concourse H

There are four other Clubs, operated by MIA—two of which are open to all travelers. These "Aviation Clubs" are located at the entrances of both Concourses B and D. They are largely under-utilized but both are comfortable and almost insulated from the terminal hubbub. The Airport Club and Club America are open to first class and business passengers but you must get a referral from your carrier. They are located in the Concourse E entranceway.

Baggage Storage

Lockers are located at all entranceways. Rates: $.75/24 hrs. Baggage check rooms on the ground level are open 24 hours. Rates start at $1.

Banks

Barnett Bank is located near Concourse C. Open M–F, 9 a.m. to 4 p.m.; Sat., 9 to noon.
Foreign exchange facilities are located throughout the terminal complex. The one at Concourse E is open 24 hours.
ATMs are located at Concourse C, upper level.

Business Services

At present, Hotel MIA at Concourse E has copying and fax facilities available free to guests but for a charge to others. MIA plans to open a full-service business center by the third quarter of 1989.

Cocktail Lounges

Food and beverage concessionaire Dobbs House has spent $13 million refurbishing the lounges and restaurants throughout the complex. Most of the 14 lounges are open until 11 p.m. A beer will run $2.60. Two mixed drinks, the Miami Breeze and the Whammy, are $5.50 keep-the-glass choices.

Gift Shops/Newsstands

MIA has over 60 shops, which carry everything from Florida glitz to high quality imported goods. You can buy a Dolphin cap at SportsPort at Concourse H for $8, or wear home a guayaberra from the men's apparel shop near Concourse E for $31.50; or you can ship home a bushel-and-a-half deluxe assortment of subtropical fruits for $67 plus freight. The Casual Approach is a women's boutique with several locations.

Hotel

Hotel MIA, a 260-room complex, is located at Concourse E. Corporate rates start at $69 (or you can rent a presidential suite for $500.) Twelve-hour stays are possible during the day ($48). All rooms are sound-proofed. The hotel is in the process of installing an executive spa-type recreational complex, complete with a nearly half-mile long jogging catwalk, pool, racquetball court, and a weight room on the rooftop. Completion date is September, 1989. Call 1–800–327–1276, or 1–800–421–0694 (FL).

Information/Assistance

A 24-hour multilingual booth is centrally located at the entranceway of Concourse E and is open daily. Information assistance phones are located on pillars throughout the complex.

Military Services

There are no separate military services at MIA.

Miscellaneous Services

Barber/Beauty shop: Concourse E. Open daily,
6:30 a.m. to 10 p.m.; Sun. 9 a.m. to 5:30 p.m. A
haircut starts at $8.
Nursery changing rooms: Concourse E and in the
International Terminal.
Pharmacy: Located between Concourse D and
Concourse E. Pharmacists' hours are daily, 9 a.m.–
5 p.m.; on call around-the-clock.
Video game room: Concourse H.

Restaurants/Snack Bars

Delis, seafood bars, buffeterias and food kiosks/carts
abound here. Prices are relatively high ($5.25 for 6
oysters; $.90 for a cup of coffee) but that doesn't stop
the sale of 8,200 hot dogs a day at $2.38 each. The
snack bar at Concourse C is open 24 hours; most
others close at 9 p.m., depending on traffic. Top of
the Port, a fine-dining restaurant on the rooftop of
Hotel MIA is open for breakfast, lunch, and dinner.
It's pricy, so ask for a window view.
For a sweet treat try the Cookie Monster ($2.45) at the
Concourse H Ice Cream Parlor. All ice cream is made
on the premises.

Post

A full service post office is located on the lower level,
Concourse B. Open M–F, 8:30 a.m. to 9 p.m.; Sat. 8:30
a.m. to noon.

Time to Kill

1 hour . . . 2 hours . . . A MIA Aviation Historical
exhibit is located at the entrance of Concourse E. Or
you can ride out to the International Terminal and go
onto the fourth level sundeck and watch flight
operations. The Concorde lands here three times a
week.

3 hours . . . You could take a Red Top limo tour
(minimum charge: $120) or take a taxi and head

downtown to shop. Miami's Bayside is a shopper's mecca on the water. Browse at the international shops, dine at one of the many elegant restaurants or just watch the cruise ships going in and out of the harbor as you prowl the Bay Walk. Or, if you're of a sporting bent, both the Miami Jai-Alai fronton and the Flagler Kennel Club are but short taxi-rides from MIA. They are seasonal so check at the Ground Transportation Centers in the lower levels first.

4 hours . . . The Metro Dade Cultural Center, located downtown, has a Fine Arts Center and the South Florida Historical Museum. It's open daily except Monday. Call 375-1700. And if you've made it this far, ride the Metromover. For $.25 you get a fast automated rail tour of the downtown business district.

For additional information call the Greater Miami Chamber of Commerce, (305) 350-7700.

MINNEAPOLIS/

ST. PAUL

MINNEAPOLIS/
ST. PAUL INTERNATIONAL AIRPORT

A frequent flyer of our acquaintance routes himself through this airport every chance he gets. For good reason: it's safe (pilots consistently rank it one of the world's safest), efficient, and homey (yep . . . that's a McDonalds). One MSP official summed it up: "We're not flashy, but we are good."

MSP is located at Wold-Chamberlain Field. Ernest Wold and Cyrus Chamberlain were two Minnesotoans killed in aerial combat in WW I.

Movie buffs will find MSP familiar. Exterior scenes of the 1969 movie "Airport" were filmed here.

The moving walkway in the Gold Concourse is the longest in the world—700 yards!!!

That large mural you see on the end of the Northwest Airlines hangar once made the Guiness Book of World Records as the largest in the world. It has since been displaced. (See DTW.)

MSP sits on the site of a former auto race track. The track operated from 1914–1916.

QUICK CONTACTS
Medical. . . . 726–1771
Police. . . . 726–5115
Lost & Found. . . . 726–5141
Information . . . 726–5555
Paging . . . Airlines

THE BASICS

Name: Minneapolis St./Paul International Airport
　　　Wold Chamberlain Field

Airport Code: MSP

Mailing Address: Lindbergh Terminal Building
　　　　　　　　St. Paul, MN 55111

Location: approximately 12 miles from
　　　　　Minneapolis/St. Paul

Telephone: (612) 726–5577

Time: Central

Daily Passengers (Rank): 48,929 (22)

Supervising Body: Metropolitan Airports Commission

AIRLINES	TELEPHONES	CONCOURSE
Air Ontario/ Canada	726–5800	Red
America West	726–1004	Green
American	332–4168	Blue
Bemidji	1–800–332–7133	Green
Braniff	1–800–272–6433	Blue
Continental	332–1471	Red
Delta	1–800–221–1212	Blue
Eastern	726–5695	Blue
Great Lakes	726–5230	Green
Mesaba NW Air Link	726–5891	Gold
Midway	1–800–621–5700	Blue
Midwest Aviation	726–9102	Green
Northwest	726–1234	all
Pan Am	1–800–221–1111	Blue
Piedmont	726–5323	Blue
Simmons	726–1234	Green
Time Air/Can. Pacific	1–800–426–7000	Red
TWA	333–6543	Red
United	726–5071	Blue
USAir	726–5356	Blue

FINDING YOUR WAY AROUND

Four concourses radiate from the two-level Lindbergh
Terminal. Concourses are color-coded and so

designated (Red, Green, Blue, Gold). Concourses have moderate travelers services; most of the airline ticket counters and enhanced amenities are on the upper level of the Lindbergh. The lower level is primarily baggage claims and ground transport. The Hubert H. Humphrey Terminal is used for international arrivals. Only the Gold Concourse has a moving walkway.

INFORMATION FOR THE HANDICAPPED

MSP provides facilities for handicapped and elderly travelers in accordance with standards established by the Architectural and Transportation Barriers Compliance Board. All travelers with special needs are advised to make arrangements with their carrier ahead of time. MSP has a TDD unit at the Travelers Aid station on the upper level, Lindbergh.

GROUND TRANSPORTATION

An airport shuttle connects the Lindbergh Terminal with the Humphrey Terminal. It's free and runs every 10 minutes. Only taxis and bus service are available at the Humphrey Terminal. All other transportation facilities are on the lower level of the Lindbergh Terminal.

Buses

A number of companies offer service for points throughout Minnesota. The Metropolitan Transit Commission buses serve Minneapolis/St. Paul and pick up in front of both terminals on the lower level. Buses #7C and #7E run every 45 minutes. The fare is $.75/off peak, $.90/peak. Bus #35P is the express and runs every 30 minutes. The fare is $1.

Car Rentals

A shuttle bus system operates every 4 to 8 minutes from the ground floors of both terminals to the car rental complex beyond the parking lots. On-site agencies are:

Auto Host	726–5017	Hertz	726–1600
Avis	726–5220	National	726–5600
Budget	726–9258		

Hotel Shuttles

Thirty-two hotels offer courtesy shuttle service for guests. Courtesy phones are on the lower level of Lindbergh.

Taxis/Vans

A cab dispatcher is on the lower level of Lindbergh. Downtown Minneapolis fare/$20; St Paul/$13. Call 726–5118. A number of vans provide transport throughout Minnesota. For transport to Minneapolis, call 726–6400. Vans run daily until midnight every 15 minutes. Fare is $6.50. For transport to St. Paul, call 726–5479. Fare is $5.50.

Parking

Short-term: $.75/first 30 mins., $.50/each additional 30 min., no maximum. Garage lot: $3/1st hr, $.75/each additional hr.
Econolot: $1/1st hr., $.50/ea. additional hr., $6/daily max. Long term indoor: $13/daily; long term outdoor: $10/daily.
Humphrey lot: $6/daily.

TRAVELERS SERVICES

You won't find elaborate shops and candlelight dining at MSP; but the shops and eating places are adequate for most travelers needs.

Airline Clubs

Delta's Crown	Blue Concourse, Gate 50.
Northwest's World Club (2)	Red Concourse, Gate 21; Gold Concourse, Gate 6.

Baggage Storage

Coin lockers are on all concourses. Rate: $1/24 hrs. Bromen's Luggage Masters is a baggage repair service located on the Lindbergh lower level.
TeleTicket also has baggage/garment storage.

Banks

Metrobank, upper level, Lindbergh. Hours: lobby, M–F 7:30 a.m. to 4 p.m.; walk-up hours,
4 p.m. to 6 p.m.
Foreign Currency Exchange in both terminals. Hours dependent on international traffic.
Automatic Teller Machines (ATMs) in both terminals.
American Express Cash Express: upper level, Lindbergh.

Business Services

TeleTicket Business Center is on the upper level, Lindbergh. It offers a variety of services, including fax, copying, notary, word processing. Private offices available, $5/hr.; conference rooms, $7/hr. Call 726–9338.

Cocktail Lounges

Eleven in the Lindbergh complex; one in Humphrey. Weekday hours, 8 a.m. to midnight, Sunday, 10 a.m. to midnight. Most lounges have a sports theme and large-screen TVs.

Gift Shops/Newsstands

Among the 16 gift shops and newsstands are: Touch The Earth, which specializes in Native American items including authentic Indian headdresses; and The Art Gallery, which offers limited edition prints. Both are in Lindbergh, upper level.

Information/Assistance

Travelers Aid booth on upper level, Lindbergh. Hours: M–F, 8 a.m. to 8 p.m., S–Sun., 11 a.m. to 8 p.m. Call 726–9435.

Miscellaneous

Game Rooms: Upper level, Lindbergh. Open 24 hours.
Hairport: Barber-beauty shop, upper level, Lindbergh. They also do garment pressing. Hours: M–F, 7 a.m. to 8 p.m.; Sat., 8 a.m. to 6 p.m., Sun., 10 a.m. to 8 p.m. Regular haircut is $10.

Nursery change room: Upper level, Lindbergh.
Shoeshine: Upper level, Lindbergh.

Military Services

Servicemen's Center, Inc.: Upper level, Lindbergh,
near Gold Concourse. Open 24 hours, daily. Call
726–9156.

Restaurants/Snack Bars

MSP has five restaurants and delis, a frozen yogurt
stand, the usual compliment of snackbars, and yes a
McDonalds—one of only three at airports in the U.S.
and as such ranks in the top 1 percent in volume,
moving about 1,000 burgers and 400 cups of coffee a
day. It's on the Gold Concourse and open from 6 a.m.
to 10 p.m. daily. The Garden Restaurant on the upper
level of the Lindbergh is open daily, 7 a.m. to 9 p.m.

Post

Mail drops and stamp vending machines are near the
entry of Gold, Blue, Green concourses; 2 are near the
central stairway of Lindbergh upper level.

Time to Kill

1 hour . . . A replica of the "Spirit of St. Louis" hangs
from the upper level of the Lindbergh, near the Gold
Concourse. The Lone Eagle was a native of
Minnesota.

2 hours . . . MSP publishes a self-guided tour of
airport facilities, complete with diagrams of planes.
Pick one up at the administrative office on the
mezzanine level of Lindbergh. The tour takes about
90 minutes.

3 hours . . . 4 hours . . . Historic Ft. Snelling is almost
within rifle shot of MSP and one of the public buses
will get you there in about five minutes. The oldest
buildings in Minnesota are here. Hours 9 a.m. to
4:30 p.m. daily. Admission is $3. During spring and
summer various re-enactments are staged.

For additional information, call the Minnesota Office
of Tourism: 1–800–328–1461 (U.S.) or
1–800–652–9747 (MN).

NEW YORK

JOHN F. KENNEDY INTERNATIONAL AIRPORT

JFK is a giant complex, covering 4,930 acres of the southeastern section of Queens with 22 miles of taxiways, 9 miles of runways and over 16,000 parking spaces. The size of Manhattan Island from the battery to midtown; it is a city in itself.

Originally known as New York International Airport at Idlewild, New York's airport opened its doors in 1948 and was rededicated to John F. Kennedy in 1963. It is located approximately 15 miles or $28 plus tolls from the "Big Apple."

Ranked 7th worldwide in passenger volume, over 30 million people traipse through JFK annually and that includes one third of all international passengers arriving in the U.S. JFK Airport accomodates 79 airlines with flights to over 150 domestic and international cities.

JFK has the world's largest Animal Port. It is operated by the ASPCA and is open 24 hours. In case you are curious; to board a dog is $13/day, a cat is $9/day and for your pet lion it's $125/day.

One rather unusual passenger arriving from a foreign destination was an American Eagle. He had gone astray in flight and landed off the Emerald Isle. Aer Lingus was kind enough to return him to us.

QUICK CONTACTS
Medical. . . . 656–4333 (Emergency)
              656–5344 (24 hr. clinic)
Police. . . . 656–4668
Lost & Found. . . . 656–4120

Information. . . . 656–4444
Paging. . . . Airlilnes

THE BASICS

Name: John F. Kennedy International Airport
Airport Code: JFK
Location: 15 miles southeast from midtown
            Manhattan
Mailing Address: John F. Kennedy International
                 Airport
                 Building 141
                 Jamaica, NY 11430
Telephone: (718) 656–5526
Time: Eastern
Daily Passengers (Rank): 82,719 (7)
Supervising Body:
The Port Authority of New York and New Jersey
One World Trade Center, 65N
New York, NY 10048

AIRLINE	TELEPHONE	LOC
Aer Lingus	(212) 557–1110	EWD
Aeroflot	(212) 397–1663	PA
Aerolineas	(212) 974–3370	EWD
Air Afrique	(212) 247–0100	WWD
Air America	(800) 247–2475	EA
Air Atlanta	(800) 241–5408	PA
Air France	(212) 247–0100	WWD
Air India	(212) 751–6400	WWD
Air Jamaica	(212) 421–9750	EWD
Alitalia	(212) 582–8900	WWD
Allegheny Commuter	(212) 736–3200	BA
ALM-Antillean	(800) 327–7230	EWD
American West	(800) 247–5692	TWA-D
American	(212) 431–1132	AM
American Eagle	(212) 431–1132	AM
American Trans Air	(718) 917–6066	UN
Arista	(718) 917–5500	BA
Avensa	(212) 956–8500	EA
Avianca	(212) 246–5241	PA

AIRLINE	TELEPHONE	LOC
Balair	(212) 581–3411	WWD
Bar Harbor	(212) 986–5000	EA
Braniff	(800) 272–6433	NW
British Airways	(212) 687–1600	BA
BWIA	(800) 327–7401	WWD
CAAC	(212) 371–9898	PA
China Air	(800) 227–5118	EWD
Condor	(800) 782–2424	EWD
Continental	(800) 525–0280	EA
Czechoslovak	(212) 682–5833	NW
Delta	(212) 239–0700	NW
Dominicana	(718) 459–5720	WWD
Eastern	(212) 986–5000	EA
Ecuatoriana	(800) 328–2367	WWD
Egypt Air	(718) 997–7700	EWD
El Al	(212) 486–2600	WWD
Finnair	(212) 889–7070	UN
Guyana	(718) 657–7474	EWD
Iberia	(718) 793–3300	EWD
Icelandair	(718) 917–0640	EWD
Japan	(212) 838–4400	EWD
Key	(718) 917–6630	EA
KLM	(212) 759–3600	EWD
Korean	(800) 223–1155	EWD
Kuwait	(212) 308–5454	EWD
LACSA	(718) 656–2555	EWD
Lan Chile	(800) 225–5526	EWD
LOT Polish	(212) 869–1074	PA
LTU	(800) 421–5842	EWD
Lufthansa	(718) 895–1277	EWD
Martinair	(516) 627–8711	EWD
MGM Grand Air	(800) 422–1101	NW
New York Helicopter	(800) 645–3994	TWA-INT
Nigeria	(212) 935–2700	WWD
Northwest	(718) 767–6868	UN
Olympic	(212) 838–3600	UN
Pakistan	(212) 370–9158	WWD
Pan American Dom.	(212) 687–2600	PA
Pan American Intl.	(212) 687–2600	PA
Piedmont	(212) 489–1460	TWA-INT
Piedmont Commuter	(800) 251–5720	TWA-INT
Princeton Airlink	(609) 924–5100	TWA-INT
Quantas	(800) 227–4500	AM
Rich International	(212) 995–3624	EA

AIRLINE	TELEPHONE	LOC
Royal Air Maroc	(800) 223–5858	EWD
Royal Jordanian	(212) 949–0050	WWD
Sabena	(212) 936–7800	AM
SAS	(718) 657–7700	WWD
Saudia	(212) 758–4727	NW
Spandax	(212) 582–8267	PA
Swissair	(718) 995–8400	WWD
TAP-Air Portugal	(212) 944–2100	EWD
Tarom-Romanian	(212) 687–6013	PA
Tower Air	(718) 917–8355	EA
TWA Domestic	(212) 290–2141	TWA-D
TWA International	(212) 290–2141	TWA-INT
United Airlines	(212) 867–3000	UN
USAir	(800) 428–4322	BA
Varig	(212) 682–3100	EWD
VIASA	(718) 656–7655	WWD
Yugoslavian	(212) 246–6401	PA
Zambia	(800) 223–1136	EWD

(AM-American, BA-British Airways, EA-Eastern, EWD-East
   Wing Departure (IAB), NW-Northwest/Delta, PA-Pan
   American, TWA-Domestic, TWA-International, UN-
   United, WWD-West Wing Departure (IAB).

FINDING YOUR WAY AROUND

A huge circular complex, JFK is comprised of 8
individual terminals; American, United, Eastern,
Northwest/Delta, Pan American, TWA International,
TWA Domestic and British Airways and one central
terminal (International Arrivals Building). Unless you
are a marathon runner, or you happen to have a
connection in a terminal nearby, you must use the
free terminal bus service. It runs every 5 to 15
minutes and takes approximately 30 minutes to
complete a full circle. The Port Authority of New York
publishes a handy guide, "Getting Around JFK" and
for the foreign traveler, "Welcome." Contact the Port
Authority for a copy of either one.

INFORMATION FOR THE HANDICAPPED

Facilities for the handicapped at JFK are in accordance
with the standards set by the Architectural and
Transportation Barriers Compliance Board. We
emphasize notifying the airline you are traveling with

JOHN F. KENNEDY AIRPORT

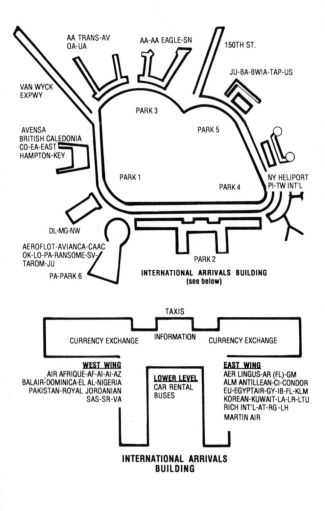

ahead of time if you need special assistance. JFK
offers a guide with information for the handicapped
or elderly titled, "Getting Around JFK, EWR, LGA."
Write to the airport or call (212) 961–5797. TDDs are
available by contacting Airport Aides or personnel at
the Information counters. For additional service call
656–5526.

GROUND TRANSPORTATION

Transportation services are as vast as JFK itself—
everything from the subway to helicopters. A
consolidated ground transportation counter (GTC) is
located on the first floor lobby of the International
Arrivals Building and on the arrivals level of each
terminal except Eastern. Personnel can assist travelers
regarding transportation. For additional information
and assistance call
(718) 656–4520.

Buses

Public Transport:
Q10/Green Bus Lines: $1 (exact change) Service to
Queens with connection to the subway. Call 995–4700
Q3/NYCTA: $1 (exact change) Service to Queens with
connection to the subway and other buses. Call 330–
1234
Express Service:
Carey Airport Express: $8/one way to Manhattan. 6
a.m. to midnight. Call 632–0500/05071
Olympia Trails: $5/one way to Manhattan. 8:45 a.m.
to 8:30 p.m.
JFK Express: $6.50/one way to Manhattan. 5:30 a.m.
to 12:30 a.m. (MTA bus/JFK Express train.) Call 858–
7272.
Minibus:
Abbey's Transportation: $11/person to midtown
Manhattan. Call 361–9092
Giraldo Limousine Service: $11–$15/person to
midtown Manhattan. Call 757–6840
Inter-Airport Connection (La Guardia or Newark)
Carey Transport: (718) 632–0500.
Salem Transport: (718) 656–4511 (Newark)

Car Rentals

A rental car counter or courtesy phone is located at each terminal's arrival level (usually near baggage claim).

Avis	656–5266	Hertz	656–7600
Budget	656–6010	National	632–8300
Dollar	656–2400		

Helicopter Service

Service is available between JFK and midtown Manhattan and is $58/one way. The helicopter departs from the TWA Terminal—Gate 37. Call (800) 645–3494

Taxis/Limos

Taxis are located at all terminals.
Rates: to mid-Manhattan $28 + tolls
       to LaGuardia $15
       to Newark $43 + $10 + tolls
A surcharge of $.50/trip is added to Newark 8 p.m.–6 a.m. and all day Sunday.
Problems: Call 869–4237
Lost & found: Call 869–4513
Limos: All Terminals (Contact GTC or use courtesy phones)
Airlimo Long Island: Call 995–5592
Transport/Classic Limousine: Call 832–5466

Parking

Hourly: Parking Lot #6—Pan Am Rooftop
$3/2 hrs. or partial
$2/each additional hr.
$24/24 hrs. max.
Short-term: Lots #1,2,3,4 and 5—Central Terminal Area
$3/2 hrs.
$1/each additional hr.
$12/24 hrs. max.
Long-term: Lots #8 and 9 (2½ miles from the Central Terminal)
Free shuttle (24 hrs.) every 10 minutes from 6 a.m. to a.m.
Every 30 min. 1 a.m. to 6 a.m.
$2/12 hrs.

\$1/each additional hr.

\$5/24 hrs./max.

For additional information, call (212) 495–5400 or (718) 656–5699.

Handicapped Parking: Special reserved parking in all lots. In Lot #5, there are 5 spaces reserved for the severely handicapped with free transportation provided to all terminals (Autolink Service). Use the courtesy phone to arrange for pick-up, dial 65009. Advanced arrangements with airlines are suggested.

TRAVELERS SERVICES

JFK is modernizing its facilities to change its lackluster appearance and enhance the existing amenities. Presently, JFK offers 58 shops, 22 airline lounges, a dental clinic, a pharmacy, a kennel and some very tasty eating establishments.

Airline Clubs

Too numerous to list and the frequency of change is high. Contact the individual airline you are traveling with or ask at ticketing.

Baggage Storage

There are two locations on the second floor of the International Arrivals Building and one location on the third floor of the Pan Am

Terminal: Call 656–8617 or 995–2228.

Hours: 1 a.m. to 10 p.m.

1 suitcase-\$3.25 (1–24 hrs.)

Lockers are located in all terminals.

Banks

Citibank: A full-service bank is located in the IAB (mezzanine area). M–W, 11 a.m. to 5 p.m. and Th–F, 9:30 a.m. to 5 p.m.

Citibank: Foreign Currency Exchange is located in the IAB (International Arrivals Building).

7:30 a.m. to 11 p.m.

West End: 1:30 p.m. to 7:30 p.m.

East End: 9 a.m. to 9 p.m.

American Terminal: 7:30 a.m. to 7 p.m.

Deak Perera International: Foreign Currency

Exchange is located in the IAB.
ATMs:

United Terminal	TWA-Domestic
American Terminal	International Arrivals
TWA-International	Building

Business Services

None

Cocktail Lounges

Cocktail lounges are located in all terminals.

Gift Shops/Newsstands

For the Yuppie and IP (impersonating Yuppie); the
Bloomies Express boutiques at the International
Arrivals Building (east wing-second level) and the Pan
Am Terminal (past security, gates 1–7) offer signature
items from the famous Bloomingdales. For the thick
hardcover to impress your neighbor on the plane,
Benjamin Books and Airport Book Shops have full
service bookstores in Terminals A and B. Century
Stores in Terminal A and in the North Terminal
present a hodgepodge of gift items for the traveler
who wants anything, and for the more discriminating
buyer Western Gift Shops (East wing-IAB) display
unique jewelry and antiques.

Hotel

International Hotel: Use free courtesy phone or call
(718) 995–9000
Rates: Single/weekday or weekend—$110
Double/weekday or weekend—$135
Hotel Reservation desk is located at the International
Arrivals Building. It is staffed 24 hours a day and they
will make reservations for you. (718) 995–9292

Information/Assistance

Counters are located at all the terminals except
Northwest/Delta. During the peak hours bilingual
personnel are available. For information over the
phone call 656–4520.
Travelers Aid: International Arrivals Building
10 a.m. to 7 p.m., M-F
3 p.m. to 7 p.m., S-Sun.

For additional information call 656–4870.
Volunteers are located in the other terminals.
Travelers Aid offers assistance to travelers including
handicapped, elderly or children over 12. They will
also aid passengers who have connections in other
terminals and those in crisis.

Military Services

No USO but the Pan Am Terminal has an Army
Liaison. Call 917–1698.

Miscellaneous

Animalport: Holding and boarding facilities for your
pet. Open daily. Call 656–7817.
Chapel: Tri-faith (located near the center of the
airport, from IAB through parking lot #2).
Catholic Chapel: 656–5348
Jewish Synagogue: 656–5044
Protestant Chapel: 656–5693
Dental Service: Suite 2311, 2nd floor/east wing of the
International Arrivals Building.
M and W, 10 a.m. to 5:30 p.m.
Th, 10 a.m. to 3:30 p.m.
Call: 656–4747
Pay TVs: Located in all terminals except United and
Eastern.
Shoeshine: Located in all terminals except Northwest/
Pan Am.
Barbershop/Beauty: Located in IAB, Eastern and Pan
Am. Shampoo and cut (male or female) will cost
about $20.
Nursery: 2nd floor of IAB.
British Airways Terminal/Trans World (Restricted to
ticketed passengers).
Pharmacy: Located in the International Arrivals
Building (2nd floor/north wing). A pharmacist is on
duty daily from noon to 9:30 p.m. The pharmacy is
open from 7:15 a.m. to 9:30 p.m. For further
information, call 656–3649.

Post

Mail boxes and stamp vending machines are located
in all terminals. Postal Annex: IAB (east wing).

Restaurants/Snack Bars

Major renovations have improved the eating establishments at JFK. For a quick pick-me-up try the espresso and a homemade cookie or brownie at Rogers Cookies of New York (International Arrivals Building). For the more health oriented, Grove Nature Snacks featured throughout JKF offers a variety of fruits and nuts that even Euell Gibbons would have been excited about. The International Buffeteria (IAB Terminal—3rd Floor) will satisfy the hungry appetite with an all-you-can-eat spread at a reasonable $11.95. If you are not up for a feast you can order a la carte. At the American Terminal, the Prop Room features pasta, fish and chicken at similar prices.

TIME TO KILL

1 to 3 hours. . . . Take a tour of the gallery at JFK. This may not be the Metropolitan Museum but it could be a wing. An impressive collection of art work is on display in the east and west wings of the International Arrivals Building. The gallery of contemporary art includes sculpture, oils, acrylics, and tapestries. And not to drop names but . . . Joan Miro, Gabrielle Roos, Salvador Dali, Alexander Calder, Jerry Okimoto, Janet Fish, Arshile Gorky, Pablo Picasso are only a few of the artists represented here. All are located on the second level except for Alexander Calder's mobile which is suspended over the lobby. The best part is it is open 24 hours.

To leave JFK and venture into the city you'll need more than 4 hours. The JFK Express will only cost $6.50 but will take 1 hour, one way. So unless you have a lengthy layover or are planning a stopover in New York you will be confined to the airport. If you are planning a stopover, the Port Authority of New York publishes an interesting brochure, "Stopovers in NY and NJ." For information call 1–800-STA-Over or (212) 481–1182.

For additional Information call:
NY Convention and Visitors Bureau. (212) 397–8222 or 397–8200.

NEW YORK

LaGUARDIA AIRPORT

In the year 1939 LaGuardia Airport opened for business. Hardly earth-shaking news when you consider that Hitler invaded Poland and World War II began that year. In New York, the Worlds Fair opened with Roosevelt on the first TV broadcast and the Yankees won the World Series.

Named after Fiorella LaGuardia, the diminutive but mighty mayor of New York, it was one of the first airports to offer amenities for the traveler. By 1940, LaGuardia was the busiest airport in the world.

Although JFK and Newark are nearby, LaGuardia is still bustling. It ranks 10th world-wide (over 66,000 passengers daily), just under San Francisco.

LaGuardia is situated on what used to be the Gala amusement park. The first building was the Overseas Terminal, known today as the Marine Air Terminal. It was located right on the edge of the bay to accommodate the era's Flying Clippers.

The Marine Air Terminal is a national historic site; domed, this building-in-the-round contains an interesting painting and story. From 1938 to 1942 artist James Brooks painted a circular frieze for the interior of the Marine Air Terminal, depicting the history of aviation. During the McCarthy era, the painting was covered over for being too "red." It appears to have had an occasional hammer and sickle. Years later during renovation work, the painting was discovered and the same Mr. Brooks restored the painting.

QUICK CONTACTS

Medical. . . . 476–5575 Weekdays 8 a.m. to 4 p.m.
Emergency: 476–5115
Police. . . . 476–5115
Lost & Found. . . . 476–5115
Information. . . . 476–5000
Paging. . . . Airlines

THE BASICS

Name: LaGuardia Airport
Airport Code: LGA
Location: 8 miles from New York
Mailing Address: Grand Central Parkway
                 Flushing, NY 10371
Telephone: (718) 476–5072
Time: Eastern
Daily Passenger (Rank): 66,372 (10)
Supervising Body: Port Authority of New York & New
                  Jersey

AIRLINE	TELEPHONE	LOCATION
American	(800) 433–7300	CTB-1
American Eagle	(800) 433–7300	CTB-1
Brockway Air	(212) 489–1460	CTB-1
Continental	(800) 525–0280	CTB-3
Midway Metrolink	(800) 621–5700	CTB-1
Piedmont	(212) 489–1460	CTB-1 and 2
Air Canada	(212) 869–1900	CTB-2
Allegheny Commuter	(212) 736–3200	CTB-2
Pennair	(212) 736–3200	CTB-2
Southern Jersey	(212) 736–3200	CTB-2
United	(212) 867–3000	CTB-2
US Air	(212) 736–3200	CTB-2
Braniff	(800) 272–6433	CTB-3
Midwest Express	(800) 452–2022	CTB-3
Pan American	(800) 221–1111	CTB-3
Pan American Express	(800) 221–1111	CTB-3
TWA	(212) 290–2121	CTB-3

AIRLINE	TELEPHONE	LOCATION
Eastern	(212) 986–5000	CTB-4
Delta	(212) 239–0700	DLT
Northwest Orient	(800) 225–2525	DLT
Business Express	(800) 345–3400	DLT
Bar Harbor	(212) 925–8113	CAT
Catskill	(800) 252–2144	CAT
Precision-Eastern Express	(212) 986–5000	CAT
East Hampton Air	(516) 537–0560	MAT
Long Island Airlines	(718) 476–5333	MAT
Resorts International	(800) 772–9000	MAT

FINDING YOUR WAY AROUND

LGA's Main Terminal is arranged in a semi-circle with four fingers (1–4) projecting from it. The lower level is for arrivals and ground transportation services while the upper level is for departure with ticketing and concessions. Airline clubs are located on the third level. Three additional Terminals (Eastern Commuter, Eastern Shuttle and Delta/Northwest) and the Marine Air Terminal complete the airport complex.

INFORMATION FOR THE HANDICAPPED

LGA meets all standards required by the Architectural and Transportation Barriers Compliance Board. If you require additional assistance, notify the airline you are traveling with ahead of time. TDD's are located on the east and west corridors of the Main Terminal. LGA offers a guide with information for the handicapped or elderly titled, "Getting Around JFK, EWR, LGA." Write to the airport or call (212) 961–5797.

GROUND TRANSPORTATION

Consolidated Ground Transportation counters (GTC) are located throughout LaGuardia to assist the

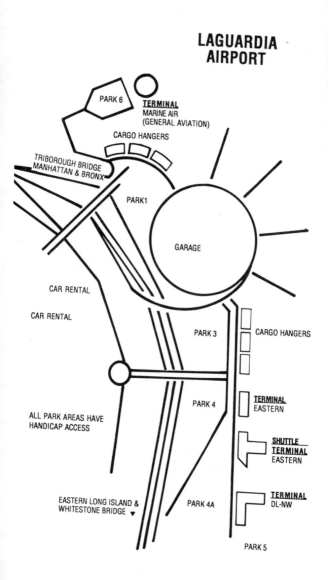

LAGUARDIA AIRPORT

PARK 6

TERMINAL
MARINE AIR
(GENERAL AVIATION)

CARGO HANGERS

TRIBOROUGH BRIDGE
MANHATTAN & BRONX

PARK1

GARAGE

CAR RENTAL

CAR RENTAL

PARK 3

CARGO HANGERS

ALL PARK AREAS HAVE
HANDICAP ACCESS

PARK 4

TERMINAL
EASTERN

**SHUTTLE
TERMINAL**
EASTERN

EASTERN LONG ISLAND &
WHITESTONE BRIDGE ▼

PARK 4A

TERMINAL
DL-NW

PARK 5

NEW YORK CITY

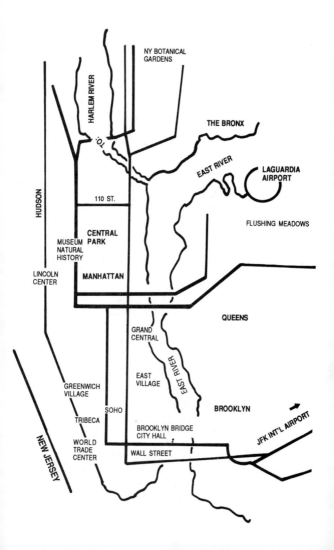

traveler. Four GTC's are located in the Main Terminal,
1 GTC at the Eastern Airline Shuttle, 1 GTC at the
Delta Terminal and 1 at the Pan Am Shuttle. For
additional information call (718) 476–5157 (7:30 a.m.
to 11:30 p.m.) or 1–800-AIR-RIDE.

Airport Shuttles

Free shuttle service (yellow and white buses) runs
between terminals every 10 to 15 minutes, 5 a.m. to
2 a.m.
Eastern runs a shuttle between the Main Terminal and
Eastern Terminal every 15 minutes, 7 a.m. to 11 p.m.
Pan Am runs a free shuttle between the Marine Air
Terminal and all terminals every 20 minutes, 7 a.m. to
10 p.m.

Buses

Q-33 Bus: (718) 335–1000
Service to Queens and connection to subway
(E,F,GG,N, and #7 trains). Departs every 10 to 20
minutes. Fare: $1 (exact change).
Q-48 Bus: (718) 330–1234
Service to Queens and Long Island Rail Road
Flushing Station. Departs every 15 minutes. Fare: $1
(exact change).
Express Service:
Carey Airport Express: (718) 632–0500
$6 one way to Manhattan, $4 one way to Queens. The
bus for Manhattan departs every 20 to 30 minutes,
6:45 a.m. to midnight. The bus for Queens departs
every 30 minutes, 6:30 a.m. to 11:00 p.m.
Olympia Trails: (212) 964–6233
Minibus:
Abbeys Transportation: (718) 361–9092
$8/person. Schedule varies according to passenger
demand. Dropoff at major Manhattan hotels. Contact
GTC for arrangements.
Giraldo Limousine: (212) 757–6840
$8 to $15/person. Schedule varies according to
passenger demand. Drop-offs between 14th and 90th
St. Contact GTC for arrangement
Inter-Airpot Connection: Carey Coaches (718) 632–

0500 Service to Kennedy Airport, 6:30 a.m. to 11 p.m. every 30 minutes. Fare is $7.

Car Rentals

Each terminal contains a car rental counter or courtesy phone.

Avis	(718) 507–3600	Hertz	(718) 478–5300
Budget	(718) 639–6400	National	(718) 803–4101
Dollar	(718) 779–5600		

Ferry

The Pan Am Water Shuttle: (212) 687–2600 or 1–800–54-FERRY. $20/one way, $38/round-trip. Operates from Marine Air/Pan Am Shuttle and Pier 11 in downtown Manhattan. Call for the schedule.

Hotel Shuttles

There are several hotels very close to the airport. Courtesy phones are located on the arrivals level (baggage claim area). A hotel reservation desk is located in the American, TWA and Eastern arrivals area of the Main Terminal and the Delta and Eastern Shuttle Terminals. Call (718) 476–5587.

Taxis/Limos

Taxis: Available at each terminal.
Fares: LGA to mid-Manhattan: about $15 plus tolls.
LGA to JFK: $15.
LGA to Newark: about $30 plus $10 tolls.
Group rates: Contact Taxi Dispatch Services, Inc. at the taxi stands. Fare ranges from $7 to $9 (plus tolls)/person. Call 784–4343.

Parking

There are 3 types of parking facilities: 1) metered parking by Marine Air Terminal, Main Terminal, and Eastern/Delta Terminals, 2) outdoor lots by all terminals and 3) a parking garage serving the Main Terminal. Free bus shuttles from lots 1, 3, 4, 4A, 5 and Delta, Eastern and Eastern Commuter to Main Terminal from 5 a.m. to 2 a.m. For additional parking information, call 429–5380. For current parking and road status, call 476–5105.

Metered Parking: $.25 each 10 minutes. Maximum parking time is 2 hrs.
Lots & Garage: $15 max./24 hrs. Up to 2 hrs./$3. $1 each hour or part until maximum. As a new idea, LGA has installed centralized pay stations. Your Visa and Mastercard will be accepted for payment. For parking information call (718) 476–5105.
Disabled Parking: Designated spaces are available. Fee is the same as above. For additional information call (212) 466–7503 or (718) 656–5072.

TRAVELERS SERVICES

Renovations are underway to upgrade LaGuardia. Meanwhile, amid the noise and rubble, there are full-service restaurants run by Marriott, and some interesting concessions and services.

Airline Clubs

American Airline's Admiral Club	3rd. floor (Room W307)
TWA Ambassador's Club	3rd. floor (Room 3771)
Eastern Airline's Ionosphere	3rd. floor (Room 3771)
USAir Club	3rd. floor (Room 3760)

Baggage Storage

Delta Terminal: Mutual of Omaha's Travel counter is located on the second floor. Hours: 6 a.m. to 8 p.m. M–F., 7 a.m. to 3:30 p.m. weekends. Call (718) 651–6725 or 478–1414.
No Lockers. After a bombing in 1975 the lockers were removed.

Banks

Manufacturers Hanover: Main Terminal (Arrival Concourse)
ATMs: Main Terminal (Departure concourse), Eastern Shuttle Terminal and PanAm/Delta Terminal.
Foreign currency exchange: #1,2,4, Delta/Northwest Terminal.

Business Services

Mutual of Omaha: Delta Terminal (2nd level).
Typing, stenography, faxing, copying machines. Call
478–1414.

Cocktail Lounges

All Terminals. In the Main Terminal, new lounges
named "Broadway," "Central Park," and "Wall Street"
conjure up images of the Big Apple. They offer light
fare, good drinks and interesting surroundings.

Gift Shops/Newsstands

The Grove is a fruit and nut concession. Eat them
there or ship them somewhere. A "Grove" is located
on each finger of the Central Terminal.
Want a companion on your flight home? At Lobster-
to-Go (a concession at LGA) you can pick your own
live lobster from a tank at a mere $10.95/lb. Or if you
don't want to boil a buddy, try taking home
chocolates instead. The same concession sells them.
(The chocolates move faster than the lobsters.)

Information/Assistance

An "AppleAides" desk staffed with senior citizen
volunteers to assist passengers is centrally located on
the departure level (second floor), Main Terminal.
Hours: M–F, 9 a.m. to 8 p.m., Sun., 2 p.m. to 6 p.m.
Closed on Saturday.

Military Services

No USO facilities.

Miscellaneous

Barbershop: Main Terminal. Shampoo and cut (male
or female) is $20.
Child Center: Main Terminal. A nursery is located in
the woman's room with changing tables. Take an
escalator to second floor and pick up free coloring
books and crayons for your toddler at the information
counter in the central lobby. Across from the same
information counter is Kidsport, a fun room for kids.
Pay TV: $.25—Main Terminal.
Pharmacy: Located on the 2nd Level of the Main

Terminal. Hours: 7:30 a.m. to 9 p.m. M–F, Sun.,
7:30 a.m. to 7 p.m. Sat. Call 429–7508.
Shoeshine: Main Terminal, Eastern and Delta/
Northwest. Cost: $2.

Post

Located on the lower level of the Main Terminal in the
central lobby area. Hours: 9 a.m. to 3 p.m., M and T
9 a.m. to 4 p.m., W, Th., F.
Call (718) 429–5689.

Restaurants/Snack Bars

The Terrace Restaurant (4th floor of Main Terminal) is
being revamped. New decor and cuisine should make
this restaurant worth trying. Or if you are in the
neighborhood (Marine Air Terminal), try Rocco's
Flying Clipper Restaurant. It offers reasonable prices
and good food with interesting surroundings that
highlight the flying clipper era.
Ice Cream: Delta/Northwest Terminal.
Fruit & Nut Stands: Main Terminal.
Coffee/Snacks: All terminals except Marine Air.

TIME TO KILL

1 to 2 hours. . . . You could pull out your book, or
visit the lobsters. Or you could catch an airport
shuttle to the Marine Air Terminal for a quick glimpse
of the "Flight." A circular frieze, 12' × 3" and 235' in
circumference, this painting was rediscovered in the
70's. Look for the controversial "red" items that
stirred the imagination and anger of McCarthy
fanatics.

3 HOURS. . . . Take an express bus and see the Big
Apple. Granted, you don't have a great deal of time
but a cruise about the city might be fun.

4 Hours or More. . . . Museums, parks, shops,
restaurants, and interesting architecture—it's all here
for the exploration and most of it is free. Contact your
visitors information center for brochures and
assistance.

For additional information call the NY Convention &
Visitors Bureau. (212) 397–8222 or 397–8200.

NEWARK

NEWARK INTERNATIONAL AIRPORT

Built on 68 acres of swamp, Newark International Airport was the first commercial airport to serve the New York and New Jersey metro area. Opened in 1928, it is 20 years older than JFK and 10 years older than LaGuardia. Smack in the center of the New Jersey industrial area and a mere 16 miles from midtown Manhattan, Newark International is a convenient alternative to its sisters JFK or LaGuardia.

EWR is approaching 60 years old and no one will deny that it needs a facelift. Plans are underway to improve the road system as well as the facilities and services at EWR, but give this aged beauty some credit. Newark is still a well-designed, clean and efficient airport.

Newark International was the first airport to boast paved runways, a control tower, a weather bureau, and a post office.

Over 23 million people passed through EWR last year, ranking Newark Airport just under Miami International in passenger volume.

Newark International now stretches over 2,300 acres and employs approximately 14,000 people. Together, Newark, JFK and LaGuardia generate $19 billion to the economy of the region.

In 1972, a mural comprised of ten panels was discovered under layers of housepaint at the old Newark Terminal. It was painted by Arshile Gorky, a leader of abstract expressionism. Only two panels remain and they are housed at the Newark Museum.

QUICK CONTACTS

Medical. . . . 961–2525
Police. . . . 961–2235 or 961–2233 (Emergency)
Lost & Found. . . . 961–2235
Information. . . . 961–2000
Paging. . . . Airlines

THE BASICS

Name: Newark International Airport
Airport Code: EWR
Location: 3 miles southwest of Newark; 16 miles
    southwest of New York.
Mailing Address: Newark International Airport
      Newark, NJ 07114
Telephone: (201) 961–2000
Time: Eastern
Daily Passenger (Rank): 63,112 (12)
Supervising Body: The Port Authority of
      New York/New Jersey
      One World Trade Center, 65N
      New York, NY 10048

AIRLINE	TELEPHONE	TERMINAL
Air Canada	869–1900	A
Allegheny Commuter	662–3201	B
American/ American Eagle	643–0304	A
Bahamasair	435–7191	A
Catskill Airways	430–3930	B
City Express	1–800–387–3060	C
Condor	1–800–782–2424	B
Continental	596–6000	C
Continental Express	1–800–525–0280	C
Continental (Shuttle)	1–800–525–0280	C
Delta	622–2111	B
Eastern	621–2121	B

AIRLINE	TELEPHONE	TERMINAL
Eastern Express-Bar Harbor	621–2121	B
Eastern Express-Precision	621–2121	B
Holiday	961–2770	B
Mall Airways	961–4865	A
Midwest Express	961–2268	A
Northwest	1–800–225–2525	A
Piedmont	624–8311	A
Piedmont Commuter	1–800–251–5720	A
TWA	643–3339	A
United	624–1500	A
USAir	622–3201	B
Virgin Atlantic (Arrivals)	242–1300	C
Virgin Atlantic (Departures)	242–1330	A

FINDING YOUR WAY AROUND

Newark International is arranged in a circular configuration with three independent terminals designated as A, B and C. Projecting from each of the terminal buildings are satellites. The upper level (departure area) of each terminal is airline ticketing and the lower level is ground transportation. The concourse level (halfway between lower and upper levels) is for passenger services. The circular satellites are utilized for flight activity and service facilities. International flights arrive at Terminal C.

INFORMATION FOR THE HANDICAPPED

Services and facilities for the handicapped at Newark comply with the standards set by the Architectural and Transportation Barriers Compliance Board. For any additional assistance, contact your airline. There is also a pamphlet available with more detailed information on the facilities at JFK, LGA and EWR.

NEWARK INTERNATIONAL AIRPORT

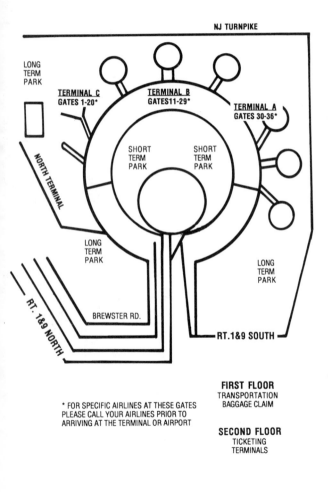

* FOR SPECIFIC AIRLINES AT THESE GATES
PLEASE CALL YOUR AIRLINES PRIOR TO
ARRIVING AT THE TERMINAL OR AIRPORT

FIRST FLOOR
TRANSPORTATION
BAGGAGE CLAIM

SECOND FLOOR
TICKETING
TERMINALS

Write to the Airport Port Authority or call (201) 961–2154. For TDD's, contact airline personnel.

GROUND TRANSPORTATION

Ground Transportation Counters (GTC) are located in the baggage claim areas of Terminals A and B, next to door #8 (lower level-arrivals) in Terminal C. Connections to the trains (Airlink) run from the nearby city of Newark.

Airline Shuttles

Free shuttles run every 10 minutes, 24 hrs./day. Pickup is at the lower level (door 6) between Terminals A, B and C. For connections between the Central Terminal Area (A, B and C) catch the bus (brown and white) on the upper level (outside door 6 or 7).

Buses

Express Service:
NJ Transit Express: (201) 460–8444 or (800) 772–2222. Fare: $7. Runs every 15 to 30 minutes, 25 hrs./day. Departs for the Port Authority Bus Terminal (42nd St. and 8th Ave.).
Olympia Trails Express Bus: (201) 589–1188 or (212) 964–6233. Fare: $7. Departs for downtown Manhattan and midtown Manhattan. Runs every 10 minutes from 5 a.m. to midnight.

Rail Connections:
Airlink Bus: (201) 460–8444. Fare: $4. Departs for Newark Penn Station. Runs every 20 to 30 minutes from 6 a.m. to 2 a.m.

Minibus:
Giraldo Limousine: (212) 757–6840. Fares: $13 to $18. Departs from all terminals. Drop-off: Between 32nd St. and 90th St. Schedule varies. Arrangements are made at the Ground Transportation Counter (GTC).

Newark Airport Limo and Car Service: (201) 242–5012. Shared transportation. Fare: $20. Drop-offs: Between Battery Park and 59th St.

Newark International Airport/NYC Minibus: (201)
961–2535. Fare: $12. Departs from all terminals.
Schedule varies. Drop-offs: Major Manhattan hotels.
Arrangements are made at the Ground Transportation
Counter.

Inter-Airport Connections:
Salem Transportation (201) 961–4250 or (718) 656–
4511. Departs every 30 to 60 minutes from 1 p.m. to
8 p.m. Fare: $18 to Kennedy Airport.
Additional Connections available to JFK or LGA.
Olympia Trails: (201) 589–1188
N.J. Transit: (201) 460–8444.

Car Rentals

Car rental counters are located at the arrival level near
the baggage claim area of Terminals A and B. Direct
phones are located at Terminal C.

Avis	961–4300	Hertz	621–2000
Budget	961–2990	National	622–1270
Dollar	824–2002		

Hotel shuttles:

To call for hotel shuttles, use the courtesy phones
located at the arrival level of each terminal.

Taxis/Limos

Stands are located at the arrival level of Terminals A,
B and C.
Taxis: Downtown and midtown Manhattan—fare: $27
to $30, plus tolls.
To city of Newark—fare: $10 to $14.
Limos:
Airport Jet Express: (201) 621–2501 or (800) 328–1919
Airport Limousine Express: (201) 621–7300 or (800)
624–4410
Carters Executive Limousine: (201) 267–0545
Newark Airport Limousine: (201) 242–5012
VIP Limousine: (201) 289–3600

Parking

Short-Term: Lots A, B and C—Central Terminal Area.
Fare: $2/1 hr., $2/ea. additional hr., $48/24 hrs.

Daily Parking: Lots A, B and C—Central Terminal Area.
Fare: $2/1 hr.; $1/each additional hr.; $18/24 hrs.
Long-Term: Lots D, E and F—Central Terminal Area.
Fare: $3/12 hrs. or part; $1/ea. additional hr.; $5/24 hrs.
Parking Information: (201) 961–2154.

TRAVELERS SERVICES

Like its neighboring airports JFK and LGA, EWR is being refurbished and the services and amenities are improving. One of the more exciting additions is Continental's Terminal C. There have been some dramatic changes to modernize this terminal. Color video monitors located throughout the terminal display airflight information and beautiful atriums and cascading waterfalls enhance the interior. Passengers traveling with children will be delighted with the two play areas staffed by Continental personnel and another new addition—changing rooms in womens and mens restrooms.

Airline Clubs

Continental's President's Club	Terminal C
Delta's Crown Room	Terminal B (Near Gate 7)
Eastern's Ionosphere	Terminal B (Departure Area)
TWA's Ambassador	Terminal A (Concession Level)

Baggage Storage

Lockers are located in Satellite B1, B2, and B3 (Terminal B). Luggage can be stored maximum 24 hours at $.50/hr.

Banks

First Fidelity Bank: Terminal A (8:30 a.m. to 3 p.m., M–F), Terminal B (9 a.m. to 3:30 p.m., M–F).
Foreign Currency Exchange: Terminals A, B, C.
ATMs: Terminals A and B.

Business Services

None available.

Cocktail Lounges

All terminals.

Gift Shops/Newsstands

For devotees of the printed word, Benjamin Books is located in Terminal A and the Airport Book Shop is in Terminal B. Both are full-service book stores. Newsstands can be found in every terminal. For a gifts-for-everyone kind of store, visit Century Shop in Terminal A. It features everything imaginable: handblown glass, silver jewelry, pewter figurines, Nientendo cartridges and even battery-operated portable TVs, a black and white costs approximately $200 and a color costs approximately $350. That's not even the tip of the iceberg.

For the sports enthusiast there is Sportsport in Terminal B. It is filled with souvenir items, sports memorabilia and other top quality sports related merchandise. It is a definite homer for you sports fans.

Hotel

Newark International Airport Marriott is located in the Central Terminal Area. There are 414 rooms and banquet/convention facilities are available. Weekday rate for a single/double is $75; weekend rate is $142 for a single and $167 for a double. For reservations call (201) 961–2860.

Additional hotels are located nearby. Courtesy phones are located throughout the arrivals level in Terminals A and B.

Information/Assistance

Information/assistance counters are located in Terminals A and B, near doors 5 and 6 on the lower level (arrival) and in Terminal C, next to exit door #8.

Military Services

None available.

Miscellaneous

Barbershop: Terminal B
Chapel: Non-denominational, open 24 hours, located in Terminal C.
Nursery facilities: Changing facilities are located in the womens restrooms on the concourse level in Terminals A and B. They are also located in men's and women's restrooms in Terminal C.
Pharmacy: Terminal B. Hours: 10 a.m. to 2 p.m., M–F.
Shoeshine: Terminal A and Terminal B.

Post

Mail slots and stamp vending machines are located in all terminals.

Restaurants/Snack Bars

The food concessions at Newark are being upgraded. At Terminal C, an atrium with 3 waterfalls will highlight a food court and selections will be from popular franchises. Don't be surprised to find the Colonel sitting next to Ronald McDonald under the Golden Arches—right out of franchise fairyland. Terminal A also has a food court complex where you can be tempted by a variety of offerings.

TIME TO KILL

1 hour. . . . Terminal A presently has student art work displayed. If your hunger for food is stronger, trek over to Terminal C. You can sit in pleasant surroundings and tempt your tastebuds.

2 or 3 hours. . . . Take a 20 minute ride by taxi to the Newark Museum. Originally founded as a museum of art, science and industry it is renown for its Tibetan collection and its fine examples of American art. Although construction has presently closed the main museum, it will reopen in the fall of 1989. In the meantime, you can wander through an authentic Victorian mansion, the Ballantine House, or visit the mini zoo where various habitats of the world are represented. Both are part of the museum complex and are free. Open from noon to 5 p.m., T–Sun. (201) 596–6550.

Or . . . If the sights and sounds of the Big Apple call you, grab an express bus. Approximately $7 and 30 minutes later you can find yourself atop the World Trade Center. The observation deck is open from 9:30 a.m. to 9:30 p.m. and there are shops galore in the main concourse. Call (212) 466–4170.

4 or more hours . . . The Meadowlands Sports Complex is a giant sports facility with a stadium, arenas and a race track. For box office information on sporting and concert activities, call (201) 935–3900 and for the race track, (201) 935–8500. It is approximately 12 miles from Newark.

Or. . . . Right next door to the Meadowlands at the Teterboro Airport is the Aviation Hall of Fame, a museum honoring the people who contributed to the history of aviation. Open daily from 10 am. to 4 p.m. Call (201) 288–6344.

For additional information contact the Visitors Information counter in Terminal A or call (201) 622–4937.

ORLANDO

ORLANDO INTERNATIONAL AIRPORT

Orlando International Airport is airy and spacious, but cozy. Huge skylights above the Great Hall of the Main Terminal bask travelers without baking them.

Orlando's code, MCO, is a holdover from McCoy Air Base, predecessor of the current facility. McCoy was named for Colonel M. N. McCoy who was killed in a plane crash in 1957.

MCO's area is 10,640 acres, making it the second largest airport in the U.S. (behind Dallas-Ft. Worth). About half the acreage is a natural preserve.

Orlando is the thunderstorm capital of the world, one reason why MCO's arrival/departure rate is near the bottom for major airports.

The first simultaneous landings of Concordes took place here in 1982. The occasion marked the opening of Disney's Epcot.

MCO is the only airport with a greenhouse—a necessity to care for the over 17,000 plants inside the terminal.

QUICK CONTACTS

Medical. . . . 0 (white phones)
Police. . . . 826–2075
Lost & Found. . . . 826–2111
Information . . . 826–2000
Paging. . . . 0

THE BASICS

Name: Orlando International Airport
Airport Code: MCO
Location: 10 miles southeast of Orlando
Address: One Airport Boulevard
            Orlando, FL 32827–4399
Telephone: (407) 826–2001
Time: Eastern
Daily Passengers (Rank): 40,825 (20)
Supervising Body: Greater Orlando Aviation
                        Authority

AIRLINES	TELEPHONES	TERMINAL
Air New Orleans	1–800–525–0280	B
Allegheny Commuter	1–800–428–4253	A
American	896–2334	A
Bahamasair	1–800–222–4262	B
British Airways	1–800–247–9297	B
Continental	1–800–525–0280	B
Delta	849–6400	B
Eastern	843–7280	A
Ecuatoriana	1–800–328–2367	A
Florida Express	859–5959	B
Icelandair	1–800–223–5500	A
Midway	1–800–621–5700	A
New York Air	1–800–221–9300	B
Northwest	351–3190	B
Pan Am	422–0701	A
Piedmont	828–6370	B
Sun Coast	1–800–541–5387	A
TWA	351–3855	A
United	859–0710	B
USAir	1–800–428–4322	A

FINDING YOUR WAY AROUND

Two Airside Terminals (designated A and B) are
joined to the Main Terminal by automatic shuttle cars.
Each Airside has basic amenities, but the Main
Terminal has more complete services. The Main
Terminal has three levels with most services clustered

in the Level 3 Great Hall. Signs are plentiful and easily understood. You can't get lost here. And if you do, pick up one of the white, in-terminal phones located on just about every pillar.

INFORMATION FOR THE HANDICAPPED

MCO conforms to Architectural and Transportation Barriers Compliance Board standards. A TDD unit is located at the Information kiosk in the center of the Great Hall.

GROUND TRANSPORTATION

All transportation facilities are located on Level 1, with the exception of public bus transport at curbside, Level 2. A "rate bank" of fares for all modes of transportation is on Level 2.

Buses

Grey Line buses load at Level 1. Fare to Disney World: $10/adult; $6/child.
Shuttle vans to Disney World: $11/adult; $6/child.
Public bus from Level 2 every 30 minutes. Downtown Orlando fare is $.75.

Car Rentals

All agency counters are located in Level 1.

Avis	851–7600	Hertz	859–8400
Budget	850–6749	National	855–4170
Dollar	826–3088	Superior	857–2023

Hotel Shuttles

Courtesy phones are in Level 1, both A and B side.

Taxis

Average fare to downtown Orlando/$24; to Disney World/$34.

Ashtin Leasing	851–3812	Yellow	422–4561
Town & Country	828–3035		

Parking

Not many parking garages have waterfalls, but MCO does. Short-term rate: $1/45 mins.; Long-term: $2/8 hrs. East (E) Lot Park and Ride (free shuttle) $1/8 hrs., $3 daily max. For parking information, call 826–2458.

TRAVELERS SERVICES

Nothing fancy here but enough to satisfy basic travel needs. All shops are centered in the Great Hall.

Airline Clubs

Continental's President	Great Hall, "A" side
Delta's Crown	Airside B
Piedmont's Presidential	Airside A

Baggage Storage

Catos: Great Hall, 6 a.m. to midnight, 7 days. $1–$3/ 24 hrs., depending on size.
Coin lockers throughout complex, $1/24 hrs.

Banks/Currency Exchange

Sun Bank: Great Hall, M–W, Sat., 8 to 5 p.m.
          Th–F, 8 to 6 p.m.
Wharton-Williams/Genesis Travel Currency Exchange in kiosk (Great Hall). T–Sat., 7 a.m. to 9 a.m., Sun.– M, 6 a.m. to 10 p.m.
Automatic Teller Machines (ATM) are behind information booth in the Great Hall.

Cocktail Lounges

One lounge in each Airside, plus one at entrance to Marketplace. Hours vary, depending on traffic.

Gift Shops/Newsstands

Located in both Airsides, Great Hall.
Benjamin Books is open daily, 7 a.m. to 10 p.m.

Information/Assistance

Kiosk in center of Great Hall at Airside shuttle exits. Hours: daily, 7 a.m. to 11 p.m.
Both Disney World and Sea World have information booths in the Great Hall.

Miscellaneous

Barbershop: Great Hall, M–F, 8:30 a.m. to 8 p.m.; Sat– Sun., 8:30 a.m. to 5 p.m.
Chapel: Great Hall, non-denominational, no services.

Conference rooms: Located on Level 2, $100/day, reserve two weeks ahead. Located on Level 2. Call (407) 826–2001.
Game room: Great Hall, 8 a.m. to midnight.
Nursery/Changing Rooms: In Airsides only.
Shoeshine: Airsides and Great Hall.

Post

Mini-post office with stamp/envelope vending machines are located in Great Hall; each Airside also has stamp vending machines and mail drops.

Restaurants

Each Airside has a full-service restaurant/snack bar. The Orlando Marketplace in the Great Hall centers a variety of offerings by concessionaires: Oriental, seafood, delis, etc. Hamburger, fries, and soda is $3.91; entrés at Beauregard's in the mezzanine start at $8.95, although for $5.95 you can sample that uniquely Floridian delicacy—gator tail. A beer is $2.50. The food is good and reasonably priced. Seating is a problem.

TIME TO KILL

1 Hour. . . . Study Duane Hanson's bronze "The Camper" long enough and you'll walk away saying "He lives." You'll find him behind the information kiosk in the Great Hall.

2 Hours. . . . If you feel vigorous and the weather is nice, stroll out to B-52 Memorial Park. It's free and open until 6 p.m., M–F.

3 Hours . . . 4 Hours . . . Orlando is covered up with theme parks that take days to see. If you just want a taste, try Disney World's World Village at Lake Buena Vista. Open daily, 10 a.m. to 10 p.m., the Village has over 45 shops and restaurants, the latter ranging from snackbars to sit-downs serving lobster and prime rib. Admission is free.

For additional information, call the Orlando Visitors Center, (407) 351–0412.

PHILADELPHIA

PHILADELPHIA INTERNATIONAL AIRPORT

Philadelphia Mayor W. Wilson Goode said in the Spring of '88: "The most serious problem facing the airport today is the lack of airfield capacity . . . (PHL) has emerged as one of the busiest facilities in the US, with passenger delays outpassing all but 10 airports in the country." To rectify that problem, PHL has kicked off a $465 million overhaul, which comes virtually on the heels of a $300 million overhaul in the mid-1970s. Visible evidence can be seen in the new $87 million international terminal (completion date— 1991) which will finally give PHL a Terminal A and replace the often criticized Overseas Terminal located 10 minutes away. The five-year plan also calls for a new 400-room grand hotel complex to be erected on-site.

The PHL Medical Center, located in Terminal C, treated 3,000 patients in 1988, and is credited with saving the lives of 7 cardiac arrest victims.

PHL is the Military Air Command's Northeastern Gateway for overseas flights. Approximately 250,000 military personnel are processed through PHL each year.

QUICK CONTACTS

Medical . . . 365–5350
Police. . . . 492–3103
Lost & Found . . . 492–3163
Information . . . 493–3181
Paging . . . Airlines Only

THE BASICS

Name: Philadelphia International Airport
Airport Code: PHL
Location: 7 miles southwest of Philadelphia
Mailing Address: Philadelphia International Airport
                 Philadelphia, PA 19153
Telephone: (215) 492–3181
Time: Eastern
Daily Passengers (Rank): 42,267 (26)
Supervising Body: City of Philadelphia
                       Division of Aviation

AIRLINES	PHONE	TERMINAL
Air Jamaica	1–800–523–5585	Overseas
Allegheny Commuter	1–800–428–4253	B
American	365–4000	E
American Eagle	365–4000	E
British Airways	1–800–247–9297	Overseas
Continental	1–800–525–0280	C
Delta	928–1700	E
Eastern	923–3500	C
Lufthansa	1–800–645–3880	Overseas
MAC	897–5644	D (Departures) Overseas (Arrivals)
Mexicana	1–800–531–7921	B (Departures) Overseas (Arrivals)
Midway	1–800–621–5700	C
Northwest	1–800–225–2525	E
Pan Am	1–800–223–1115	D
Piedmont	1–800–251–5720	D
TWA	923–2000	B Overseas (Arrivals)
United	568–2800	D
USAir	563–8055	B
Wings	492–2018	Gate D1

FINDING YOUR WAY AROUND

A main complex consisting of Terminals B, C, D, and E connects four concourses: B, C, D, and E, which extend from these terminals. (There is no A Terminal.) The only confusing aspect is the location of the Overseas Terminal—a mile-and-a-half away and reached by free buses.

INFORMATION FOR THE HANDICAPPED

PHL conforms to standards provided by the Architectural and Transportation Barriers Compliance Board for handicapped and elderly travelers. All passengers with special needs are advised to notify their carrier prior to departure. TDD units are located in the information booths of both the Main and Overseas Terminals.

GROUND TRANSPORTATION

All transport departs from the baggage claims areas in the lower levels. The best way to the center of the city is by the SEPTA Airport Line.

Buses/Rapid Transit

Public buses run every hour from the ground level of the terminal. Fare is $1.
Rail transportation to downtown by the Airport Line leaves from the baggage claim areas. Trains run every 30 minutes. Time to downtown: 25 minutes. Fare/$4. Call 574–7800.

Car Rentals

Agency counters are in the baggage claims areas of each terminal.

Avis	492–0900	Hertz	492–2925
Budget	492–9447	National	492–2750
Dollar	492–2692		

Hotel Shuttles

Courtesy phone banks are located in each baggage claims area.

Taxis/Limos

Taxis are dispatched from the ground level.
Approximate fare to downtown Philadelphia is $16.

Parking

Free shuttle buses link terminals to remote lots. Rates
for the short-term lots: $.50/15 mins; garage lots: $3/2
hrs; long-term, $6/daily. Call 492–3292 for parking
information.

TRAVELERS SERVICES

PHL has all the amenities, with shops offering
everything from sports souvenirs to gourmet
popcorn, plus 21 lounges and restaurants.

Airline Clubs

Delta's Crown	Concourse E
United's Red Carpet	Terminal C
Eastern's Ionosphere	Concourse C
TWA's Ambassador	Terminal B
USAir's Club	Terminal B

(Note: Lufthansa and Air France share a lounge in the
Overseas Terminal. British Airways also has a lounge
in the Overseas Terminal.

Baggage Storage

Coin lockers are located on all concourses and in the
Overseas Terminal. Rates are $.75/24 hrs.

Banks

Check cashing is available in Terminal C. Hours:
M–Sat., 10 a.m. to 7 p.m.

Business Services

Notary services are located at the check cashing
agency, Terminal C.

Cocktail Lounges

Lounges are in every terminal and generally open
from 8:30 a.m. to 11 p.m., daily. The Half-Shell in the
main terminal is a raw bar/sandwich shop.

Gift Shops/Newsstands

Men and women's clothing stores, a toy store, florists, and newsstands which stock over 250 magazine titles are here. A mini-mall of shops is at the end of Terminal D. The Brad Allen Bookstore is between Terminals B and C. Hours are daily, 7 a.m. to 10 p.m.

Information/Assistance

The Information Center is at Terminal C, second level. Hours: daily, 7 a.m. to 11 p.m.
Travelers Air is at Terminal E. Hours are daily, 7 a.m. to 10 p.m. Call 365–6525.
American Red Cross is located in the Overseas Terminal. Hours: daily, noon to 10 p.m. Call 365–7490.

Military Services

The USO is in Terminal D. Open 24 hours. Call 365–8889. Salvation Army's Red Shield Military Lounge is located on the first level, Terminal C. Open 24 hours. Call 365–7677.

Miscellaneous

Barber Shop: Terminal C. Hours: daily, 6 a.m. to 8 p.m.
Shoeshine stands: Terminals C, E.
Video arcade: Between Concourses B and C, main level.
Medical Center: Terminal C. Hours: daily 7 a.m. to 11 p.m.

Post

An automated mini-post office is located in Terminal C, second level. Mail drops are located throughout the complex.

Restaurants/Snack Bars

Fountain Court is a full-service restaurant located on the third level of the Main Terminal. Open daily, 11:30 a.m. to 8:30 p.m. Past Times Grille is a buffeteria located in Terminal C. It is open daily from 5:30 a.m. to 11 p.m. There are walk-up snack bars throughout the complex. Food courts are clustered in Terminals D and E. Hours vary based on passenger traffic.

TIME TO KILL

1 hour. . . . Aside from shopping or eating there is little to do. Like most major airports PHL closed its observation deck for security reasons.

2 hours . . . .PHL conducts tours of the facility on a daily basis. You can latch onto it by calling 492-3163. The tour takes about 90 minutes.

3 hours . . . No matter what Davy Crockett claimed, the crack in the Liberty Bell is still there. Take SEPTA to downtown Philadelphia. Open daily, 9 a.m. to 5 p.m. Admission is free. The Liberty Bell is located in a glass pavilion across from Independence Hall.

4 hours . . . Independence Hall is probably the most historic U.S. building. This is where the Declaration of Independence was signed and the Constitutional Convention met. Tours are continuous and the Hall is open daily from 9 a.m. to 5 p.m.

For additional information, call the Philadelphia Visitors Information, (215) 636-1666.

PHOENIX

PHOENIX SKY HARBOR INTERNATIONAL AIRPORT

Phoenix Sky Harbor is an oasis—an attractive and modern airport, which offers the flavor of the Southwest in its decor, fine food, and unique shops. It is one of the few airports to boast a health club where the tense traveler can unwind with a healthy workout and sauna.

Daily, PHX accomodates just over 40,000 passengers and always with a smile.

On July 16, 1935, the city of Phoenix purchased the land for the airport from the ACME Investment Company—the company that Wile E. Coyote is always buying from. It consisted of 285 acres and a few buildings. The price—$35,300 in cash and a $64,700 mortgage.

On an average day at Sky Harbor over 800 planes arrive and depart, 40,000 plus passengers enplane and deplane, and in excess of 200 tons of cargo are handled. All this activity generates approximately $25.2 million a day.

QUICK CONTACTS

Police. . . . 273–3311
Medical. . . . 273–3311
Lost & Found. . . . 273–3307
Information. . . . 275–7912 (Terminal 2) or 275–7916 (Terminal 3)
Paging. . . . 273–3300

THE BASICS

Name: Phoenix Sky Harbor International Airport
Airport Code: PHX
Location: 5 miles southeast of Phoenix
Mailing Address: 3400 Sky Harbor Blvd.
Phoenix, Arizona 85034
Telephone: (602) 273–3300
Time: Mountain
Daily Passenger Rank: 40,469 (29)
Supervising Body: The City of Phoenix

AIRLINE	TELEPHONES	TERMINALS
Air Sedona	1–800–535–4448	Exec.
Alaska	254–0303	2
American	258–6300	3
America West	894–0737	3
Braniff	244–8853	2
Continental	258–8911	3
Delta	258–5930	3
Eastern	271–0878	3
Golden Pacific	1–800–352–3281	1
Havasu Air	1–800–824–6614	1
Mesa	225–5150	1
Midway	1–800–225–2525	2
Northwest	273–7325	3
Piedmont	1–800–428–4322	2
Skywest	1–800–453–9417	3
Southwest	273–1221	1
StatesWest	220–0070	2
TWA	252–7711	2
United	273–3131	2
USAir	1–800–428–4322	2

FINDING YOUR WAY AROUND

Three independent terminals (1, 2, and 3) connected
by a walkway comprise Sky Harbor. An International
Terminal is wedged between Terminals 2 and 3.
Ground transportation services are located on the
lower levels of all terminals and concessions and
services are located on the upper level.

INFORMATION FOR THE HANDICAPPED

PHX conforms to the standards set by the
Architectural and Transportation Barriers and
Compliance Board. Notify the airline you are traveling
with ahead of time if you need special assistance.
TDD's are available in the following terminals:

Terminal 1—Budget Car Rental counter in North
 Lobby, 6 a.m. to midnight.
Terminal 2—Budget Car Rental counter in North
 Lobby, 6 a.m. to midnight.
Terminal 3—American West Airlines Passenger
 Service Office (baggage claim lower
 level). Available 24 hrs./day.

GROUND TRANSPORTATION

Ground transportation services are located on the
street level of each terminal. For additional
information or assistance call (602) 273–3383.

Buses

Phoenix Transit System (PTS): Fare to downtown is
$.75 (exact change). M–F, 6 a.m. to 8:37 p.m. Call
253–5000.

Super Shuttle: Runs 24 hours. Airport to door service.
Departs every 15 minutes to all sectors of the Valley
from 9 a.m. to 9 p.m. Airport to downtown: 1st
person, $15 to $25, additional persons, $5 to $10. Call
244–9000.

Courier Transportation: On call/24 hours. Airport to
city costs $4.50. Call 244–1818

Car Rentals

Avis	273–3222
Budget	267–4000
Dollar	275–7588
Hertz	267–8822
National	275–4771

Hotel Shuttles

A courtesy telephone center is located adjacent to the
baggage claim area in all terminals.

Taxis/Limos

Taxis: Three taxi companies operate out of Sky Harbor. Taxi and limousine service is available in the parking areas. Fares are $2.50 for the first mile and $1.20 for each additional mile. Airport to downtown costs $7, unless you hit traffic and then you could be delayed 1 hour and pay up to $18. For information or complaints, call 273–3383.

AAA Cab: 437–4000
Courier Cab: 244–1818
Yellow Cab: 252–5071/5252

Limos: Airport to downtown fare is $10 to $15. If your destination is 5 to 10 miles then the fare is $15 to $20. For rates of 3 or more in one party, add $5 to $8 for each additional person.

Parking

Parking is available adjacent to each passenger terminal. There is also garage parking next to Terminal 3. A Sky Harbor Travelers Information Service broadcasts information on parking, road and other conditions on 1610, AM.

Terminal 1	Every half hour	$.50
	24 hours (max.)	$10.00
Terminal 2	Every half hour	$.50
(Daily Rate)	24 hours (max.)	$5.00
Terminal 2	Every half hour	$.50
(Hourly Rate)	24 hours (max.)	$10.00
Terminal 3	Every half hour	$.50
	24 hours (max.)	$10.00
Shuttle Lot	Every half hour	$.50
	24 hours (max.)	$3.00

TRAVELERS SERVICES

There are some very interesting and unique stores to wander through at PHX and if you want something special to take home, you'll find it here. In addition to a variety of shops and concessions, PHX offers the executive Air Vita. It is a wonderful combination business and fitness center.

Airline Clubs

American Admiral's Club	Terminal 3
America West's Phoenix Club	Terminal 3
Continental President's Club	Terminal 3
Delta's Crown Room	Terminal 3
Northwest's World Club	Terminal 3
TWA's Ambassador Club	Terminal 2

Baggage Storage

Lockers are located in all terminals past security. Rate: $.50/day.

Banks

First Interstate Bank: Full service bank—Terminal 2
Hours: 9 a.m. to 4 p.m. M–Th,
9 a.m. to 5 p.m. F.
ATMs: Terminal 1 and 3
American Express: Terminal 2

Business Services

Air Vita is a combined fitness and business center and is located in Terminal 3 (West Mezzanine). It is open Sun to F, 6:00 a.m. to 8:00 p.m. For information call 225–5190. If you are an Air Vita member, many of the services are free or at a reduced rate. For non-members $15 will buy you unlimited use of Air Vita's exercise facilities, locker room amenities and sauna. Additional services are also available. For example, a foot massage costs $15, a full massage (45 minutes) costs $32, and for sapeborsting*, $12.
*(If you know what sapeborsting is, you deserve this one on the house.)

Cocktail Lounges

Cocktail lounges are located in all terminals.

Gift Shops/Newsstands

You've hit the mother lode at PHX. Aside from the usual airport fare you'll find: Indian jewelry (a Hopi silver bracelet will start at $50), Indian pottery (Santa Clara pottery will run from $4 to $300), Navajo sand paintings, Indian baskets, blankets and Hopi Kachina Dolls (begin at $85). The Gallery of the Southwest houses quality artwork and at what other airport can you purchase potted cactus and mounted scorpions?

Hotels

No on-site hotel. A courtesy phone center to arrange accomodations and/or shuttle transport is located adjacent to the baggage claim area of each terminal.

Information/Assistance

Tourist and Information:
Terminal 2 and Terminal 3
M to F, 9 a.m. to 9 p.m.
Sat to Sun, 9 a.m. to 5 p.m.

Military Services

No USO.

Miscellaneous

Barber Shop: Terminal 2, 8:30 a.m. to 5 p.m.
Game Room: Terminal 2 and 3, 7:30 a.m. to 9:30 p.m.
Shoeshine: Terminal 1 and 3, 7 a.m. to 9 p.m. $3/shoes and $4/boots.

Post

Terminal 3 has a full-service post office. Hours: 6:00 a.m. to 6:00 p.m. Mail drops and stamp vending machines are located in all terminals.

Restaurants/Snack Bars

A good selection and variety of food is offered at PHX. The Fuente Del Sol is an excellent full-service restaurant with continental cuisine and candle-lit service. It is open 7 a.m. to 10 a.m., 11 a.m. to 4 p.m. and from 5 p.m. to 10 p.m. The Signature Room is another fine restaurant. It is open 11 a.m. to 2:30 p.m. and from 4:30 p.m. to 9:30 p.m.

TIME TO KILL

1 hour. . . . The selection of quality shops at PHX is excellent and even if you don't want to part with that green stuff, it is a pleasure to browse through some of the stores. You could also take the time to look at

some of the artwork dispersed throughout this airport; it is of museum quality.

Or. . . . If you are a member of the Air Vita Club-you know what you can do with your spare time at PHX. A full fitness center is available along with amenities; workout clothing, shampoo, hair dryers, and sauna. Business services are also available. For the businessman who travels frequently, a membership is worth considering. Call 225–5190.

2 Hours. . . . Desert Botanical Gardens. Only 5 miles from the airport, this 3 acre botanical garden displays over 10,000 desert plants. Open daily from 9 a.m. to 5 p.m. Admission: $2.50. Call 941–1225.

Or. . . . The Phoenix Zoo is in the same neighborhood. Approximately 1,200 creatures reside on the Papago Park grounds. Open daily from 9 a.m. to 5 p.m. Admission: $5.00.

3 Hours. . . . Explore an Indian Ruin. Near the Botanical Gardens is Pueblo Grande, an Indian ruin and museum. It is open M–Sat, 9 a.m. to 4:45 p.m. and Sun, 1 p.m. to 4:45 p.m. Admission: $.50.

And located downtown, a 5 minute cab ride away, is the Heard Museum, renown for its Indian Artifact Collection and Barry Goldwater's collection of Kachina Dolls (wooden dolls invoking supernatural spirits). It is open M–Sat, 10 a.m. to 5 p.m. and Sun, 1 p.m. to 5 p.m. Admission: 3:00/adults. Call 252–8840.

4 hours. . . . The Phoenix Art Museum contains some of the finest collections of Western Art. It is open T–Sat, 10 a.m. to 5 p.m. and Sun, 1 p.m. 5 p.m. Admission: $2.00. Call 257–1880.

For additional information call the Phoenix and Valley of the Sun Convention and Visitors Bureau, (602) 254–6500.

PITTSBURGH

GREATER PITTSBURGH
INTERNATIONAL AIRPORT

Originally dedicated in 1952, Pittsburgh International
has seen three additions but very little real change in
the years since. But in the years to come that will no
longer be true. A $560 million overhaul is in the
works, including a new terminal, a 50 percent
increase in gate capacity, underground people-
movers—all to be completed by 1992. Pittsburgh the
city long ago left behind its image of rolled up sleeves
and metal lunch pails; its airport is on the verge of
doing the same.

Despite its location and image, PIT is seldom snowed
in. It is not uncommon for it to act as a reliever when
East Coast airports are blanketed in blizzard weather.

PIT is USAir's major hub. In 1986 the carrier enplaned
6 million passengers, more than all other PIT carriers
combined. USAir is also the region's eighth largest
employer.

PIT's control tower stands 227 feet tall and is the
tallest FAA built structure in the U.S., completed in
1985 at a cost of $12.5 million.

QUICK CONTACTS

Medical. . . . 778–2522
Police. . . . 778–2522
Lost & Found. . . . 778–2504
Information. . . . 778–2525
Paging. . . . Airlines

THE BASICS

Name: Greater Pittsburgh International Airport
Airport Code: PIT
Location: 14 miles west of Pittsburgh
Mailing Address: Greater Pittsburgh International Air.
Pittsburgh, PA 15231
Time: Eastern
Telephone: (412) 778–2504
Daily Passengers (Rank): 47,830 (23)
Supervising Body: Allegheny County Aviation
Department

AIRLINES	TELEPHONES	LOCATION
American	771–4437	West
Allegheny Commuter	1–800–428–4253	South
British Airways	1–800–247–9297	South
Canadian Air	391–6351	West
Christman	343–0255	West
Continental	391–6910	West
Delta	566–2100	West
Eastern	471–7100	South
Northwest	281–2088	West
Pan Am	1–800–221–1111	East
Piedmont	566–1610	East
TWA	391–3600	West
United	288–9900	East
USAir	922–7500	S,E

FINDING YOUR WAY AROUND

Most facilities are concentrated on a central dock.
Three docks–West, East, and South–branch outwards.
Southeast Dock in turn branches from the South
Dock. There are no moving sidewalks, but walking
time from one end of the complex to the other is only
about 14 minutes.

GREATER PITTSBURGH
INTERNATIONAL AIRPORT

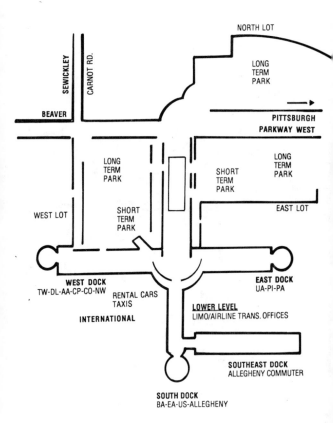

PITTSBURGH METRO AREA

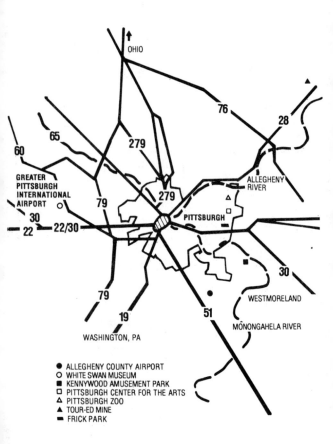

INFORMATION FOR THE HANDICAPPED

PIT provides facilities for handicapped and elderly travelers in accordance with standards of the Architectural and Transportation Barriers Compliance Board. All travelers with special needs are advised to make arrangements with their carriers. PIT publishes a "Provisions for the Disabled" brochure which is available at the Information desk. A TDD unit is located at the Business Service Center in the Main Terminal.

GROUND TRANSPORTATION

All ground transportation departs from the central lower level.

Buses

Several firms provide shuttle and limo service to downtown and throughout the suburban area. Airlines Transportation Company (471–8900) runs every 30 minutes. Fare to downtown, $8; to Oakland, $8.50.

Car Rentals

Counters are located near passenger pickup areas on the field floor level.

Avis	262–5160	Hertz	262–1705
Budget	262–1500	National	262–2312
Dollar	262–1300		

Hotel Shuttles

Courtesy phones are located at the field level of Central Dock.

Taxis/Limos

Yellow Cab (655–8100) pickup is on lower level. Fare to downtown: $25.

Parking

Super Short-Term (for pickup and delivery only) $.75 cents / 20 minutes; $24/daily max. Short-Term: $1.75/hr. Long-Term: $5.50/day. Extended Term: $4.25 / day. For parking information call 264–7490.

TRAVELERS SERVICES

Travelers amenities are basic but are improving. A bookstore, an upscale apparel shop, and a golf pro shop are all recent additions.

Airline Clubs

Delta's Crown	West Dock
Eastern's Ionosphere	South Dock
TWA's Ambassador	West Dock
United's Red Carpet	East Dock
USAir's Club	East Dock

Baggage Storage

Coin lockers are available. Rates: $.50/24 hrs.

Banks

Automatic Teller Machines are located throughout the complex. American Express is at Eastern's Ionosphere Club.

Business Services

Mutual of Omaha Business Center is located on the main floor, South Dock. Open daily, 6:30 a.m. to 10 p.m. Call 472-0241.

Cocktail Lounges

A number of lounges are located in the South, Southeast and West Docks, and in both the east and west wings of the Main Terminal. Hours: daily 10 a.m. to 11 p.m.

Gift Shops/Newsstands

The Vuarnet Shop is open daily, 8 a.m. to 9 p.m. Besides sunglasses, Vuarnet specializes in unisex wearing apparel. Benjamin Books is open daily, 7 a.m. to 10 p.m. Both stores are located in the main lobby of the Central Dock.

Hotel

The Airport Hotel is on the mezzanine level of the Main Terminal. Rates start at $50 during the week; $40 on weekends. Call 264-8000.

Information/Assistance

An information booth is located in the main lobby. It is staffed from 7 a.m. to 11 p.m., daily. Call 778–2525. Blue Airport Assistance phones are located throughout the complex. Travelers Aid (264–7110) is open 9 a.m. to 8:30 p.m. It is located on the field level of the Central Dock.

Miscellaneous

Nursery: "Kidsport" overlooks the airfield. It is located on the main floor of the South Dock. Nursing and change facilities are nearby, as well as throughout the complex.
Central Medical Center: Main floor, East Dock. Hours are 9 a.m.–5 p.m., M–F.

Restaurants/Snack Bars

Besides the usual snackbars, PIT has a fine dining facility, The Captain's Table, open daily 7:30 a.m. to 9 p.m., located in the main lobby, Central Dock. A 24-hour buffeteria is located nearby.

Post

A Post Office branch is located on the main floor. Open 8 a.m. to 5 p.m., M–F. Mail drops and stamp vending machines are located throughout the airport.

TIME TO KILL

1 hour . . . Fine tune your swing or just whack some balls at the Tee Off & Take-Off golf pro shop on the Central Dock.

2 hours . . . Hyeholde Restaurant is consistently one of Pittsburgh's top-rated dining establishments. It is a 50-year old castle-like structure with beams rescued from a 250-year-old barn. Try the Virginia Spots dinner ($22), or Framboise Ambrosia ($5.50). Reservations are recommended for dinner. A jazz cabaret in the basement plays until 1 a.m. Call 264–3116. "Hyeholde," incidentally, is Old English for "fortress on the hill." It is about 5 minutes and a $7 cab ride from PIT.

3 hours . . . Ride the Duquesne Incline to the Mt. Washington overlook of Pittsburgh. It's $.65 to the top and $.65 back down. Open until midnight every day, the view is worth the effort day or night.

4 hours . . . The Carnegie Museum of Natural History is one of the nation's finest, and is noted for its art collection, historical artifacts, and gems. It is open daily except Monday, from 10 a.m. to 5 p.m. Admission is $3.

For additional information call the Greater Pittsburgh Convention and Visitors Bureau, (412) 281–7711.

ST. LOUIS

LAMBERT–ST. LOUIS
INTERNATIONAL AIRPORT

The world's 16th largest airport, STL came close to being called CWI. In 1970, the Illinois state legislature began a lobbying effort to relocate STL to the Columbia-Waterloo area in southwestern Illinois. What became known as the Lambert Controversy raged for nearly 7 years before the U.S. Department of Transportation stepped in and settled the matter by leaving STL where it is. It was a good thing for Missouri, too. STL pumps about $2.5 billion into the local economy, providing jobs for 13,000.

STL was named for Major Albert Lambert, a local legend and aviation pioneer. Among other achievements, Lambert was the first to bomb a ship (1910), and in 1921 he bought the plot of ground that became STL.

STL became the first municipally-owned airport in the U. S. when Lambert sold his field in 1928.

The Main Terminal was built in 1956. It was the design of Minoru Yamasaki, an achitect noted for the richness of his pre-cast concrete designs. He also did the Century 21 Exposition in Seattle.

QUICK CONTACTS
Medical. . . . 426–8120
Police. . . . 426–8100
Lost & Found . . . 426–8100
Information . . . 426–8040
Paging. . . . Airlines

THE BASICS

Name: Lambert-St. Louis International Airport
Location: 10 miles northwest of St. Louis, Missouri
Airport Code: STL
Mailing Address: PO Box 10212
          St. Louis, MO 63145
Telephone: (314) 426–8000
Time: Central
Daily Passengers (Rank): 55,788 (16)
Supervising Body: City of St. Louis Airport Authority

AIRLINE	TELEPHONE	LOCATION
Allegheny Commuter	1–800–428–4253	Concourse A
Air Midwest	739–1111	D-64
American	231–9505	A-7
Comair	621–8900	A-6
Continental	241–7205	A-8
Delta	421–2600	A-4–6, D 79–81
Eastern	621–8900	A-10/15
International	423–4510	East Terminal
Jet America	429–1588	East Terminal
Northwest	241–2151	A-2/3
Piedmont	421–5027	A-6
Southwest	421–1221	East Terminal 79/81
Trans Mo	423–3414	East Terminal
TWA	291–7500	B-16–24, C-26–52, D-60–78
United	454–0088	A-12,14
USAir	421–1018	A-9

FINDING YOUR WAY AROUND

STL is comprised of a Main Terminal with four
concourses. At the farthest end of Concourse D is the
East Terminal which is used primarily for
international flights. Airline ticket counters are on the
mid-level of the vaulted Main Terminal, and both the
lower and mid-levels have snackbars, gift shops, and
lounges.

INFORMATION FOR THE HANDICAPPED

STL conforms to Architectural and Transportation
Barriers Compliance Board standards. A TDD unit is

located in the police station, mid-level, Main
Terminal.

GROUND TRANSPORTATION

All Ground Transportation facilities are located at the
lower level of the Main Terminal in front of the
Baggage Claim area.

Buses

Times/fare information is adjacent to the rental car
counters on the lower level. Use Exits 6 or 7. Time to
downtown St. Louis is approximately 1 hour. Buses
run every hour, 8 a.m. to 10 p.m. To Clayton, every
45 minutes, 6 a.m. to 5:50 p.m. The fare is $.85.

Car Rentals

Car rental counters are located between Exits 9 and 11
in front of the Baggage Claim area on the lower level.

Avis	426–7766	Hertz	426–7555
Budget	423–3000	National	426–6272
Dollar	423–4004		

Hotel Shuttles

Courtesy phones are located in the Baggage Claim
area on the lower level.

Taxis/Limos

There is an information booth at Exit 12, lower level.
The fare to St. Louis is $17; to Clayton it's $12. Taxis
allow sharing by up to 5 passengers.
Jet Port Express runs every hour to downtown. It
takes approximately 25 minutes. The fare is $6/one-
way, $9 round-trip. Call 427–8119.

Parking

Short-Term Parking Garage in front of Main Terminal,
$.50/1st hr; $1.25/1–2 hrs. Valet parking is on the
Upper Level across from the Main Terminal: $15/24
hrs. Intermediate parking is adjacent to the garage,
$2/6 hrs, $5/daily maximum. Long-term parking lots:
$1.25/6 hrs, $4/daily maximum. There are free shuttles
to the Main Terminal. Parking information is available
via radio 1120 AM.

TRAVELERS SERVICES

STL is equipped with basic travelers needs facilities.

Airline Clubs

American's Admiral	Lower Level, Main Terminal
TWA's Ambassador (2)	Lower Level, Main Terminal, Concourse C, Gate 42
Delta's Crown	Concourse A.

Baggage Storage

Coin lockers are on all the concourses. $.50/24 hrs.

Banks

Mercantile Bank is located at mid-level, near the entrance to Gates 16/24. Hours: 7:30 a.m. to 5:30 p.m., M–F., Sun 1 p.m. to 5 pm. American Express Cash Express ATM is located in the Main Terminal.

Business Services

There are no business service facilities.

Cocktail Lounges

Cocktail lounges are scattered throughout the complex. There are two on the lower level of the Main Terminal.

Gift Shops/Newsstands

Newsstands and gift shops are located throughout the complex. The Ozark Store features arts and crafts by local artisans.

Information/Assistance

There is an information booth on the mid-level at the entranceway to the Gates 16–24 concourse. Hours are daily, 10 a.m. to 8 p.m.

Miscellaneous

Barber shop/Hair salon: Mid-level. Hours: M–F, 8 a.m. to 8 p.m.
Shoeshine: Four throughout mid-level.
Game Room: Open 24 hours, mid-level.
Nursery Changing Rooms: Located on all concourses.
Chapel: Interfaith services Sunday, 2 p.m. Located in Conference Room A, mid-level.

Military Services

The James S. McDonnell USO is the largest at any airport. Open 24 hours, it is located at mid-level. There is also a military ticket counter near Exit 14, mid-level.

Restaurants/Snack Bars

Snack bars are located throughout the Main Terminal and on all concourses. Gateway Gardens is a sit-down restaurant/cafeteria on the mid-level of the Main Terminal.

Post

A full service post office is located at mid-level, Exit 6. Open 8:30 a.m. to 10:30 a.m., M–F. Stamp vending machines and mail drops are scattered throughout the complex.

TIME TO KILL

1 Hour. . . . Ever wonder why Lindbergh called his plane the "Spirit of St. Louis"? Because STL's namesake, A. B. Lambert, donated $1,000 to the Lone Eagle to construct it. A reproduction of the historic craft is on the upper level.

2 Hours . . . On the lower level, between Exits 13 and 14, is the "Aviation . . . An American Triumph" mural. Executed by St. Louis artist Siegfried Reinhardt, the 8-foot high, 142-foot-long painting, one of the world's largest, traces the history of aviation from Icarus to "Columbia."

3 hours . . . Take a tour of the Sports Hall of Fame at Busch Stadium. It's open daily, 10 a.m. to 5 p.m., March through December. The admission is $2, and for children under 12, $1.50. Call 241–3900.

4 hours. . . . On the Riverfront downtown is the Gateway Arch, one of the wonders of the modern world. Open daily but hours vary with the time of year. Call 445–4265. Admission is $2.50 and well worth it. Jetport Express will drop you off and pick you up for $9.

For additional information call the Convention and Visitors Commission, 421–1023, or 1–800–325–7962.

SALT LAKE CITY

SALT LAKE CITY
INTERNATIONAL AIRPORT

Originally a cinder-covered strip amidst a marshy pasture called Basque Flats (for the shepherds who used to roam here), Salt Lake City International Airport has come a long way from its 1911 beginnings. From 100 acres it has grown to over 7,000, and unexpected and phenomenal growth has become the standard.

SLC was originally dedicated as Woodward Field in 1920 after pilot John P. Woodward who was killed while flying an airmail route to Salt Lake City. On hand for the ceremonies was Jack Dempsey, then world heavyweight champion.

Trivia buffs take note: on May 23, 1926, two Salt Lakers climbed atop some mail sacks aboard a biplane and flew to Los Angeles. The pair's eight-hour trip was the first commercial passenger flight out of Utah.

This is Delta country. Approximately 75 percent of all passengers and flights from SLC fly Delta—a result of the 1987 merger with Western Airlines.

SLC is not only an airport, it's also a campus. A branch of Salt Lake City Community College is housed on-site.

QUICK CONTACTS
Medical. . . . 575–2405
Police. . . . 575–2405
Lost & Found. . . . 575–2425
Information. . . . 575–2400
Paging. . . . 575–2600

THE BASICS

Name: Salt Lake City International Airport
Airport Code: SLC
Location: 3 miles west of Salt Lake City
Mailing Address: AMF Box 22084
                 Salt Lake City, UT 84122

Telephone: (801) 575-2400
Time: Mountain
Daily Passengers (Rank): 27,847 (41)
Supervising Body: Salt Lake City Airport Authority

AIRLINE	TELEPHONE	LOCATION
Alpine Air	373-1508	TU-1
America West	378-0121	TU-1
American	521-6131	TU-1
Continental	359-9800	TU-1
Delta	532-7123	TU-2
Eastern	539-1100	TU-1
Horizon	1-800-547-9308	TU-1
Northwest	1-800-225-2525	TU-1
Pan Am	1-800-221-1111	TU-1
TWA	539-1111	TU-1
United	328-8011	TU-1

FINDING YOUR WAY AROUND

Two terminals, Terminal Unit 1 and Terminal Unit 2,
are joined by an outdoor walkway and upper-bridge
moving sidewalk. Baggage claims and ticketing are on
the ground floors of each terminal; escalators and
elevators connect the terminals with the four
concourses on the second level. Concourses A and B
radiate from Terminal Unit 1, while concourses C and
D extend from Terminal Unit 2.

INFORMATION FOR THE HANDICAPPED

SLC provides facilities for handicapped and elderly
travelers in accordance with standards of the
Architectural and Transportation Barriers Compliance
Board. All travelers with special needs are advised to
notify their air carriers prior to departure. TDD units

are located in the Travelers Aid booths of each terminal.

GROUND TRANSPORTATION

All transportation departs from the lower level of each terminal.

Buses

Utah Transit Authority stops at ground level in front of both terminals. Fare for the 17-minute ride to downtown is $.50. Buses depart every 20 minutes.

Car Rentals

Car rental agencies are located on the ground floor of each terminal.

Avis	539–1117	Hertz	539–2683
Budget	363–1500	National	539–0200
Dollar	596–2580		

Taxis/Limos

A number of firms provide service. Pick-up points are at the lower level. Fares start at $8.

Parking

The short-term lot is in front of the terminals. Rates: $.85/1st hr.; $.50 each additional hr.; $4.85/daily maximum. Rates for the three long-term parking lots located at the SLC entrance are: $.85/1st hr.; $.50 each additional hr.; $2.85 daily maximum. Free shuttles to and from terminals.

TRAVELERS SERVICES

Basic amenities are available, but there is very little sizzle.

Airline Clubs

Delta's Crown Room (2)   Concourse C between the connector of Concourses C & D.

Baggage Storage

Coin lockers are located throughout the complex.
First 24 hours/$.75 cents, $1 each additional 24-hour
period.

Banks

Zions Bank is a full-service bank located on the first
level of Terminal 1. Hours: M–F, 9 a.m. to
6 p.m.
An American Express ATM is located in Terminal 1.

Business Services

Fax machines are at the entranceways of Concourses
B & C. Copying can be done at the Morris Travel
Desk, Terminal 1.

Cocktail Lounges

There are only two lounges, one on the third level,
Terminal Unit 1; the other on the second level,
Terminal Unit 2. Hours are daily, 9 a.m. to 11 p.m.

Gift Shops/Newsstands

SLC's travelers amenities are standard. This is,
however, one of the very few airports in the world
where you can rent ski equipment. Canyon Sports in
each terminal provides that service.

Information/Assistance

Travelers Aid operates information booths.
Hours: M–F, 9 a.m. to 5 p.m.; S-Sun, 9 a.m. to 6 p.m.
Salt Lake County Visitors and Convention Bureau is
on the ground level, Terminal Unit 2. Hours are daily,
9 a.m. to 5 p.m.

Miscellaneous

Barbershops are located in each terminal.
Infant care centers are on the ground level, Terminal
Unit 1, and second on the second level of Terminal
Unit 2. TV lounge areas are in both terminals.

Post

Mail drops and stamp vending machines are located
in each terminal.

Restaurants/Snack Bars

The Terrace, a full-service restaurant with lounge is located on the third level, Terminal Unit 1. Hours are daily, 11:30 a.m. to 9 p.m. Cafeterias are located in each terminal and stand-up snackbars are on the concourses.

TIME TO KILL

1 hour . . . Hop off the moving sidewalks that connect the terminals and study the art/photography exhibits that line the walls. SLC has invested $350,000 in paintings, photographs and sculptures created by local artists.

2 to 3 hours . . . Take a bus or taxi to Temple Square. The Mormon Temple and the Tabernacle are here, plus museums and historic buildings. The Visitors Center will guide you. On Thursday nights the choir practices. (Note: Only Mormons are allowed in the Temple; the Tabernacle is open to all.)

4 hours . . . The Family History Center, site of the world's largest collection of genealogical archives, is open daily except Sunday. You can trace your family tree—even if your name is John Jacob Jingelheimer Schmidt. On most nights the Center is open until 9 p.m. Opening hours vary. For time schedule, call 532–3327.

For additional information, call the Utah Visitors and Convention Bureau, (801) 575–8000.

SAN DIEGO

SAN DIEGO INTERNATIONAL AIRPORT—LINDBERGH FIELD

San Diego is stretched out on the edge of the bay like a languid bather basking in the sun. It is a destination airport and not a hub like its sisters San Francisco or Los Angeles. And when your plane makes the approach to San Diego, you can understand why. Sparkling blue water dotted with sails salute you. As an airport it may lack the vitality of LAX and the diversity of SFO but it makes up for it in scenery and in convenience to its city.

On May 27, 1927, out on a small airstrip in San Diego, Charles Lindbergh cranked up the "Spirit of St. Louis" and took off on his solo flight to Paris, France. From this time on the San Diego Airport has been linked with the Lindbergh name.

The San Diego Unified Port Authorities have kept a watchful eye on their tidelands and it has paid off. San Diego Bay is noted for being the cleanest and most beautiful in the world. With increasing concerns over noise pollution, San Diego Airport was one of the first in the U.S. to establish nighttime flight restrictions.

QUICK CONTACTS

Medical. . . . 231–5260
Police. . . . 231–5260
Lost & Found. . . . 231–5260
Information. . . . 231–7361
Paging. . . . 231–5252 or Airlines

THE BASICS

Name: San Diego International Air Terminal
Lindbergh Field
Airport Code: SAN
Location: 3 miles northwest of San Diego
Mailing Address: P.O. Box 488
San Diego, CA 92212
Telephone: (619) 291–3900
Time: Pacific
Daily Passenger Rank: 27,675 (43)
Supervising Body: San Diego Unified Port District

FINDING YOUR WAY AROUND

SAN is comprised of two terminals, East and West, connected by an uncovered walkway. International flights arrive at the East Terminal.

INFORMATION FOR THE HANDICAPPED

SAN conforms to the standards provided by the Architectural and Transportation Barriers Compliance Board for elderly and handicapped travelers. Notify the airline you are traveling with ahead of time if you require special assistance. TDD's are located at the Travelers Aid station of the West Terminal and the East Terminal.

AIRLINE	TELEPHONE	TERMINAL
Alaska	800–426–0333	WT
American	232–4051	WT
American Eagle	232–4051	WT
America West	560–0727	ET
Braniff	231–0700	ET
British Airways	800–247–9297	ET
Continental	232–9155	ET
Delta	233–8040	WT
Delta/Sky West	233–8040	ET
Northwest	239–0488	WT
Pan Am	800–221–1111	WT
Piedmont	800–251–5720	ET
Southwest	232–1221	ET
Stateswest	800–247–3866	WT

AIRLINE	TELEPHONE	TERMINAL
Sun Pacific	714–7810	ET
TWA	295–7009	ET
United	234–7171	ET
United Express	234–7171	ET
USAir	574–1234	ET

GROUND TRANSPORTATION

Ground transportation is located at the East and West Terminals near the baggage claim area. The proximity of the airport to the city means inexpensive transportation. You can even walk to it. There is a beautiful walkway along the bay into the heart of the city.

Buses

San Diego Transit is located in the center traffic isle at the East Terminal and the far west end of the West Terminal. Downtown service every ½ hr. 6 a.m. to midnight. Fare: $1.

Car Rentals

Car rental counters are located in both terminals near the baggage claim area.

Avis	231–7171	Hertz	231–7000
Budget	297–3851	National	231–7100
Dollar	231–2373		

Hotel Shuttles

Courtesy phones are located at both terminals with a display board in the baggage claim areas.

Taxis/Limos

Taxi stands are across the street from the East Terminal on the second island and east of the baggage claim building at the West Terminal. There are no dispatch phones. Average fare to downtown: $1.

Limos: Old English Livery Service   223–6533
      Paul the Greek   579–0605
      Marina Limousine   222–5466

Parking

There are four parking lots close to the terminals and a long-term lot. Shuttle service is provided.

Lots 1,2,3:
$.50—First hr.
$ 1—Each additional hr.
$ 8—First 24 hr. max.
$16—25–48 hrs.
$10—Each additional 24 hr. period or any portion.
Lot 4 and Long-Term: $5 / 24 hrs. or any portion.

TRAVELERS SERVICES

Travelers services and amenities are limited here. You are very close to the city and the need for extensive services is unnecessary.

Airline Clubs

None

Baggage Storage

None

Banks:

California First Bank:
Foreign currency exchanged. East Terminal
M–Th, 8:30 a.m. to 4:30 p.m.
F, 8:30 a.m. to 6 p.m.
ATMS: East Terminal

Business Services

None

Cocktail Lounges

Cocktail lounges are located in both terminals.

Gift Shops/Newsstands

The gift shops and newsstands are standard airport fare offering just enough variety, so that if you have forgotten your toothbrush you will probably find it here. There is a duty free shop located in the West Terminal. If you are searching for some souvenirs you will find them here, but for a greater selection in shopping try the Broadway Pier. It's just a short walk from the airport.

Hotels

No on-site hotel; however the Sheraton Harbor Island East is only ½ mile from the airport. Call 291–2900.

Information/Assistance

Travelers Aid Stations—East Terminal (Baggage Claim Area) West Terminal (Central Area) Staffed 7 a.m. to 10 p.m. Call 231–7361.

Military Services

No USO. Information/Travelers Aid station in the East Terminal (central area) will assist military personnel.

Miscellaneous

Nursery: Changing facilities are provided in women's restrooms.

Post

Stamp machines and mail drops are in all terminals. Stamps may also be purchased from the gift shops.

Restaurants/Snack Bars

SAN has nothing to really brag about in the way of eating facilities. There are two restaurants (East and West terminals) open from 8 a.m. to 10 p.m. and coffee shops as well as other snack concessions.

TIME TO KILL

1 hour. . . . A breath of fresh sea air is a short walk away. Stroll along the Broadway Pier which lies south of SAN. Fine shops and restaurants abound in a park-like setting. And if that doesn't strike your fancy, relax, sit down on a bench and watch the ships. To the east is a view of the San Diego skyline and to the west is the bay.

2 hours . . . Escape the humdrum and take a ferry across to Coronado Island. Filled with interesting history, this island houses the 100-year-old Hotel Del Coronado. Marilyn Monroe filmed "Some Like It Hot" here and rumor has it that the Duke of Windsor first set eyes on Wallace Simpson at this grand hotel. Ferries run every hour daily from 10 a.m. to

10 p.m. (Embarcadero Area-Broadway Pier). The ride takes 15 minutes and costs $1.50.

3 hours. . . . San Diego Yacht Club. Home of America's Cup and the much disputed catamaran. Who knows, you may catch Dennis Conner battening down the hatches of his victorious vessel.

4 hours or more. . . . Play Dr. Doolittle and talk to the animals at the world famous San Diego Zoo. Fifteen minutes by cab. Open daily 9 a.m. to 4 p.m. Call 234–3153.

Or. . . . The Maritime Museum is only 10 minutes from the airport in the Embarcadero Area. Climb aboard any of the three historic vessels harbored there; the Star of India, the Berkeley or the Medea. Open daily 9 a.m. to 8 p.m. Call 234–9158.

For additional information call the San Diego Convention & Visitors Bureau Information Center, (619) 232–3101.

SAN FRANCISCO

SAN FRANCISCO
INTERNATIONAL AIRPORT

An airport smorgasborg, SFO reflects the cultural diversity and richness of its community. Contemporary architecture, adorned with paintings and sculpture, provides a sophisticated backdrop for the traveler. An array of excellent food concessions and interesting and unique shops complete the picture.

Although San Francisco is primarily a destination airport, approximately 83,000 people travel through here daily which places SFO 7th in the country for passenger volume.

San Francisco's humble origins begin on May 7, 1927, when the San Francisco Airport was dedicated as "Mills Field Municipal Airport of San Francisco." At the end of 1 year—22,352 arrival flights hauling 38,302 passengers generated $11,619.71 in revenue. Today? Over 230,000 arrivals, 30 million passengers, $125 million in operating revenue. Not so humble.

Because this airport and its runways are built on 2,500 acres of tidelands, constant maintenance is required— the runways have a slight sinking problem.

QUICK CONTACTS

Medical. . . . 877–0444
Police. . . . 876–2424
Lost & Found. . . . 876–2261 (Items lost in plane— contact airline)
Information & Paging. . . . 6–2377 (courtesy phone at airport) 876–2377 (outside airport) 761–0800 (San Francisco)

BASICS

Name: San Francisco International Airport
Code: SFO
Airport Mailing Address: PO Box 8097
San Francisco, CA 94128
Location: 16 miles south of downtown San Francisco
Telephone: (415) 876–2121
Time: Pacific
Daily Passenger (Rank): 83,300 (9)
Supervising Body: City & County of San Francisco

AIRLINE	TELEPHONE	TERMINAL
Air Canada	876–7485	N
Air France	877–5904	I
Alaska	877–0217	S
American	877–6150	N
American Eagle	877–6150	N
Braniff	800–372–6433	S
British Airways	877–0622	I
CAAC	392–2197	I
Canadian Airlines	800–426–7000	I
Cathay Pacific	877–0201	I
China Airlines	877–0201	I
Continental	800–525–0280	S
Delta	552–5700	S
Eastern	877–5825	S
Hawaiian	800–367–5326	I
Japan Airlines	877–3260	I
LTU International	800–421–5842	I
Lufthansa	876–7322	I
Mexicana Airlines	800–531–7921	I
Northwest	877–6941	S & I
Pan Am	877–2316	I
Philippine	877–4800	I
Piedmont	876–7201	N
Qantas	877–3840	I
Singapore	876–7372	I
Southwest	877–0222	S
TACA	800–535–8780	I
TWA	877–4222	S
USAir	877–0169	S
UTA French Airlines	877–0369	I
United	876–3069	N & I
Wardair	800–237–0314	I

FINDING YOUR WAY AROUND

San Francisco Airport contains 3 terminals: North, International and South. All terminals are bi-level with the lower level for arrivals and ground transportation services and the upper level for departures and additional services and concessions. Concourses or boarding areas (A to G) radiate from each terminal. All 3 terminals are connected by an enclosed passageway. International passengers are directed through the International Terminal.

INFORMATION FOR THE HANDICAPPED

SFO complies with the standards set by the Architectural and Transportation Barriers Compliance Board. Contact the airline you are traveling with if you need additional assistance. SFO also publishes a guide titled, "A Guide To Services For The Disabled And Elderly." Contact the airport for a copy. TDD's are located in the AT&T Communications Center (International Terminal). Daily, 8 a.m. to 10 p.m.

GROUND TRANSPORTATION

Taxis, bus and shuttle stops, and courtesy vans are located on the lower level of all terminals. SamTrans buses, rental cars and off-Airport shuttle buses operate from the upper level of all terminals. Ground transportation display boards with departure times and fares are located throughout all the terminals on the lower level and at the center islands on the lower roadway. At the North Terminal (lower level) a center kiosk offers ground transportation information.

Buses

SamTrans: Departure level (North and South Terminals). (415) 761-7000
7B: Local runs 5:30 a.m. to 1:21 a.m. (30 or 60 minute intervals). Fare to downtown: $1.00 (50 minutes)
7F: Express runs 6 a.m. to 12:55 a.m. (30 or 60 minute intervals). Fare to downtown: $1.25 (35 minutes).

SFO Airporter: Arrival level (all terminals). 673-2433. Runs from 5:30 a.m. to 2:00 a.m. Fare to downtown: downtown: $6/one way.

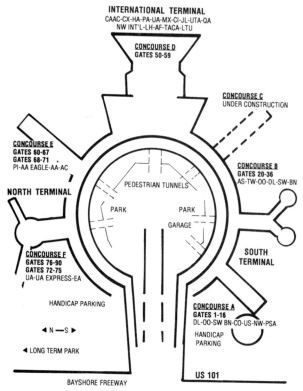

SAN FRANCISCO
INTERNATIONAL AIRPORT

INTERNATIONAL TERMINAL
CAAC-CX-HA-PA-UA-MX-CI-JL-UTA-QA
NW INT'L-LH-AF-TACA-LTU

CONCOURSE D
GATES 50-59

CONCOURSE C
UNDER CONSTRUCTION

CONCOURSE E
GATES 60-67
GATES 68-71
PI-AA EAGLE-AA-AC

CONCOURSE B
GATES 20-36
AS-TW-OO-DL-SW-BN

NORTH TERMINAL

PEDESTRIAN TUNNELS

PARK

PARK
GARAGE

CONCOURSE F
GATES 76-90
GATES 72-75
UA-UA EXPRESS-EA

SOUTH TERMINAL

HANDICAP PARKING

◄ N — S ►

CONCOURSE A
GATES 1-16
DL-OO-SW BN-CO-US-NW-PSA

HANDICAP
PARKING

◄ LONG TERM PARK

US 101

BAYSHORE FREEWAY

TO: SAN JOSE

SAN FRANCISCO BAY AREA

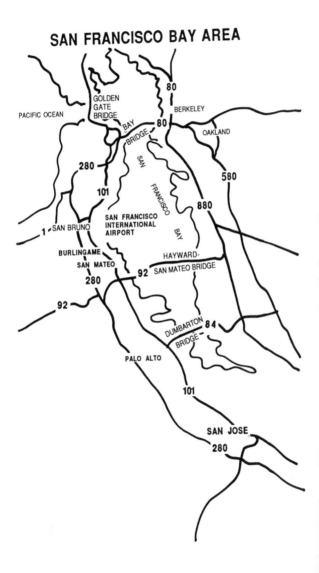

Additional public transportation is available. Check the ground transportation boards on the lower level of each terminal.

Car Rentals

Car rental counters are located in the baggage claim areas.

Avis	877–6780	Hertz	877–1600
Budget	877–4415	National	877–4745
Dollar	952–6200		

Shuttles

On-Airport Shuttle: A brown bus designated "Terminal Shuttle" operates every 5 minutes from 5:30 a.m. to 1 a.m. from the upper level roadway.
Off-Airport Shuttles:
California Mini-Bus: 775–5121
Good Neighbors AirBus: 777–4899
Lorries: 826–5950
Super Shuttle: 558–8500
Yellow Van Service: 282–7433
Francisco's Adventures: 821–0903
Airport Limo: 877–0901

Taxis/Limos

Taxis: Taxi stands are located at the center island on the lower level of all the terminals. Fare to downtown: $25. (Up to 5 passengers can ride for the price of one.) Available 24 hrs./day. For information or problems call 6–2424 (courtesy phone).
Limos: Information on limousine service is available in the baggage claim areas of all the terminals. $38/hr. (3 hr. min.) or per passenger rate of $8/hr. to downtown San Francisco.

Parking

Garage parking is located at the center of the terminal complex.
Rate: $1/1 hr., $1 each additional hour up to $11 max./ 24 hrs.
Valet Parking is available at level 4 of the garage. Rate: $16 plus garage fees. 6 a.m. to midnight. 877–0227.
Long-Term Parking is located in Lot D (north of the

terminal complex). $3/3 hrs. and $7/day. Free shuttle
service is available.
For information and parking conditions (24 hrs.) call
877–0123.

TRAVELERS SERVICES

In addition to quality shops, excellent restaurants and
eating concessions, SFO can flaunt 2 business centers,
10 nurseries, a shower, a barber/beauty shop and
several galleries and exhibits.

Airline Clubs

American's Admiral	North Terminal—Boarding E
British Airways' Captains	Intl Terminal—Boarding D
Cathay Pacific's Marco Polo	Intl Terminal—Boarding D
1st Class	Intl Terminal—departure level
China's Dynasty	Intl Terminal—departure level
Continental's President's	South Terminal—Boarding A
Delta's Crown	South Terminal—Mezzanine
Eastern's Ionosphere	South Terminal—Gate 32
Japan's Sakura	Intl Terminal—Boarding D
Lufthansa's Senator	Intl Terminal—Boarding D
Mexicana's Golden Aztec	Intl Terminal—Boarding D
Northwest Orient's Topflight	Intl Terminal—Ticket Level
Pan Am's Clipper	Intl Terminal—Boarding D

Philippine's Mabuhay	Intl Terminal—Boarding D
Qantas' Captains	Intl Terminal—Boarding D
Singapore's Silver Cris	Intl Terminal—Ticket Level
TWA's Ambassador	South Terminal—Boarding D
United's Red Carpet Room	North Terminal—Mezzanine

Baggage Storage

Baggage storage: Amlock: Located in the connector between the International and South Terminal. Hours: daily, 7 a.m. to 11 p.m. Phone: 877–0422.

Piece/day rates:		
	Carry-on—	$ 1.50
	Standard—	$ 2.50
	Oversized—	$ 3.75
	Golf bags—	$ 5.00
	Surfboards—	$10.00

Lockers are located in all the terminals (upper level) behind the ticket counter areas. $.75/day.

Banks

Bank of America: Full service bank M—F, 8 a.m. to 5 p.m.
North Terminal (mezzanine)
International (behind Pan Am ticketing).
Foreign Currency: Bank of America Branch
International: Daily, 7 a.m. to 11 p.m.
Boarding Area D: Daily, 8 a.m. to 8 p.m.
Citicorp: International (next to security check point, upper level). Daily, 7 a.m. to 11 p.m.
ATMs: All terminals.

Business Services

AT&T Business Service Center: Located at the International Terminal. Hours: Daily, 10 a.m. to 8 p.m.
It offers primarily communication services: international calls, fax machines, and conference rooms for rent ($20/hr). Call 877–0269.

Mutual of Omaha Service Center: Located at the South Terminal. M to F, 7 a.m. to 9 p.m. Sat. and Sun., 7 a.m. to 7 p.m.
Limited services: Photocopying, and faxing. Call 877-0369.

Cocktail Lounges

Some are cozy, some are designed for carousing, but the lounges at SFO are very nice. Names like the Barbary Coast, The Fog Bank and (what else) The Golden Gate are clever and inviting. The Personalities Bar in Concourse B and the Private Reserve restaurant's lounge between the International Terminal and the South Terminal are available for private parties or functions.

Gift Shops/Newsstands

This airport is a mini-shopping mall offering flowers, jewelry, clothing, porcelain, crystal, and seafood. The California Shoppe (North Terminal) sells fine wines and champagne, cheeses and other goodies from California—all wrapped and ready to go. The Western Shop (International) offers western-style clothing and gifts, and in the Locker Room (South Terminal), San Francisco's sports fans will have fun fumbling through T-Shirts and other apparel as well as souvenir items.

Hotel

Courtesy phones for hotel service are located in the baggage claim area of each terminal.

Information/Assistance

For information around-the-clock, use the white courtesy phone and call 7-0118.
Travelers Aid: Daily, 9 a.m. to 9 p.m.
North Terminal (Upper level)
South and International Terminals (Lower level).
Call 877-0118.

Military Services

USO: International Terminal (4th Floor) Daily, 24 hours.
MILPERCEN: Military Personnel Center, International

Terminal (4th floor). Daily,
24 hours. Call 877–0388.

Miscellaneous

Art Galleries and Exhibits: SFO has several exhibition
areas (2 exhibit galleries are located in the connectors
between the International and South terminals and
International and North terminals and along boarding
area F in the North Terminal). The displays change
approximately every four months and include art
work, crafts, historical exhibits, etc. There are
additional works of art—paintings, photographs,
sculpture throughout the airport. Call 876–2416

Barber/Beauty shop: Located between the North and
International Terminals. Weekdays, 7 a.m. to 6 p.m.
and Saturdays 7 a.m. to 5 p.m. Courtesy phone: 7–
0830.

Chapel: Christian Science Reading Room, North
Terminal Daily, 8 a.m. to 10 p.m. 877–0105.

Clinic: Lower level of International Terminal. Open
daily 24 hrs. A doctor is available between 8 a.m. to
1 a.m. Nurses are on staff other hours. Courtesy
phone: 7–0444. Outside phone: 877–0444.

Game Room: Located in the North Terminal (behind
Eastern ticket counter). 8 a.m. to midnight.

Nurseries: All terminals, but a larger facility is located
in the North Terminal (mezzanine level). It is open 24
hours. Courtesy phone: 6–2136.

Shoeshine: North (between Concourse E and F) and
South Terminals (Near Concourse C).

Showers: Located in the connector between the North
and International terminals. Shower with soap and
towels: $6.
Weekdays, 7 a.m. to 6 p.m.
Sat. 7 a.m. to 5 p.m.
Courtesy phone: 7–0830.

Travel Agency: Amlock Travel Services, International
Terminal Weekdays, 9 a.m. to 5 p.m. Call 877–0422.

Post

Stamp machines and mail drops are located in all the
terminals. Drops are in the ticket lobby areas near

security check points and at the HUB of the North Terminal.

Restaurants/Snack Bars

SFO's food concessions run the gamut. Succulent seafood, fresh baked sourdough and pastries, California wines and cheeses, Italian pastas and cappuccino and an orgy of oriental delights including sushi and yaki soba are only a few of the selections that reflect the influence of this ethnically rich community.

There are three full service restaurants: Terrace Room (North Terminal) 6:30 a.m. to 9:45 p.m., Private Reserve (South Terminal) 11:15 a.m. to 3 p.m. (lunch), 4 p.m. to 9:30 p.m. (dinner) and the Crab Pot (North Terminal) 7 a.m. to 10 p.m.

TIME TO KILL

1 or 2 hours. . . . San Franciscans are proud of their artistic community and international heritage. Look around you. SFO boasts that it's a gateway to the world and what an exciting entrance it is. Permanent art work surrounds you and the shops and concessions will excite even the seasoned traveler. Browse through any number of the stores (take some sourdough home), and check out the exhibits.

3 hours or more. . . . Catch an airport shuttle to the Powell-Hyde Cable Car for a thrilling 30-minute ride up and down the hills of San Francisco (including Nob and Russian Hills) climaxing at Fisherman's Wharf. If your constitution is still good, walk around the shops, restaurants, historic ships, and lounges. There is no end to the fun you can have here and to top it all off, the Golden Gate serves as a backdrop to this exciting and lively complex. The cable cars run weekdays 5:30 a.m. until 11 p.m., weekends 5:50 a.m. until 11 p.m. or later. Fare: $2. Call 673–6864

4 hours or more. . . . Take the National Park's tour of the notorious federal prison, Alcatraz. This is a self-guided tour that includes a slide show with audio narrations by former prisoners and guards.

Admission: $7 for adults and $4.50 for children. Ferries depart from Pier 41 at Fisherman's Wharf and run from 9:30 a.m. to 2:45 p.m. Call 546–2896.

One other idea. . . . Twin Peaks offers the highest and best view of the Bay Area and Grey Line runs a 3½ hour tour which includes this unforgettable sight. The Grey Line bus departs from TransBay terminal on Mission street. Call 558–9400. Fare runs $19.50.

For additional information call the San Francisco Visitors Information Center: (415) 391–2000.

SEATTLE

SEATTLE–TACOMA INTERNATIONAL AIRPORT

SEA is one of the most modern and pleasant airports in the U.S. It just recently completed a $21 million overhaul and expansion of its Main Terminal; its long-term master plan anticipates facilities for the expected 50 percent passenger volume increase before the century is out. Considering its nearly 300 percent passenger increase since its present complex was dedicated in 1973, the master plan may not be very realistic.

Because it is a gateway to the Orient, SEA not only welcomes foreign visitors in 20 languages, but also provides recorded announcements in Japanese in its transit cars.

SEA's collection of art that graces its facilities rivals Atlanta-Hartsfield in both numbers and quality. Purchased in 1970 at a cost of $300,000, the collection includes Robert Maki's "Central Plaza" sculpture, a 10,000-pound aluminum work specifically designed for SEA.

When the Seattle Sonics won the NBA championship in 1979, a record 35,000 fans mobbed SEA when the team returned from Washington, D.C.

QUICK CONTACTS

Medical. . . . 911
Police. . . . 911
Lost & Found. . . . 243–5521
Information . . . 431–4444
Paging. . . . Airlines

THE BASICS

Name: Seattle–Tacoma International Airport
Airport Code: SEA
Location: 13 miles south of Seattle
Mailing Address: PO Box 68727
Seattle, WA 98168
Telephone: (206) 433–4645
Time: Pacific
Daily Passengers (Rank): 39,577 (31)
Supervising Body: Port of Seattle

AIRLINES	TELEPHONES	CONCOURSE
AirBC	1–800–663–0522	B
America West	763–0737	A
American	241–0920	B
Braniff	1–800–272–6433	C
British Airways	1–800–247–9297	N&S Sat.
Canadian	433–5088	B
Coastal Airways	1–800–547–5022	B
Continental	624–1740	C
Delta	241–2300	B
Eastern	622–1881	C
Finnair	1–800–223–5700	N. Sat.
Harbor	1–800–521–3450	B
Hawaiian Air	1–800–367–5320	B
Horizon	762–3646	C
Japan Air Lines	1–800–525–3663	S. Sat.
Mexicana	1–800–531–7921	S. Sat.
Northwest	1–800–225–2525	S. Sat.
Pan Am	1–800–221–1111	S. Sat.
Scandinavian	1–800–221–2350	S. Sat.
Thai	467–0600	S. Sat.
TWA	447–9400	A
United	441–3700	N&S Sat.
USAir	587–6229	A

FINDING YOUR WAY AROUND

SEA consists of a Main Terminal with four concourses
designated by alphabetical letters and two satellite
terminals, North and South, all connected by an
underground automated passenger transit system. All

international arrivals deplane at the South Satellite
where U.S. Immigration and Customs facilities are
housed. Airline ticketing and most travelers services
are located on the main floor of the Main Terminal.
The lower level of the Main Terminal is for baggage
claims and ground transportation.

INFORMATION FOR THE HANDICAPPED

SEA provides facilities for the handicapped according
to standards of the Architectural and Transportation
Barriers Compliance Board. All passengers with
special needs are advised to consult with the airline
carrier prior to departure. A TDD unit is located at the
Pacific Northwest Bell Communications Center in the
Main Terminal. A brochure for travelers with special
needs is available at the Travelers Aid booth in the
baggage claims area of the Main Terminal.

GROUND TRANSPORTATION

A ground transportation information booth is located
outside the north end of the Main Terminal on the
Baggage Claims level. It's staffed daily from 7 a.m. to
2 a.m. Call 431–4444, or #46 at the courtesy phones.

Buses

Express buses leave every 15 minutes for downtown
Seattle. The fare is $5; travel time is 25 minutes.
Dispatcher: 431–5906. Metro Transit buses depart
from the south end of the baggage claims area.
Schedules are posted at the stop. For route
information call 447–4800.

Car Rentals

Six rental agencies have information counters in the
baggage claim area.

Avis	433–5231	Hertz	433–5266
Budget	443–5246	Mini-Rate	248–2442
Dollar	433–5825	National	433–5501

Hotel Shuttles

Courtesy phones for hotel/motel pickups are located
in the baggage claim area.

Taxis/Limos

Curbside telephones for taxis are located outside the baggage claim area. Rates are posted by the phones. Downtown fare is $21.

Limo service is available by pushing #46 at one of the courtesy phone centers. The average fare is $25.

Parking

SEA's parking garage can accomodate 4300 vehicles but it fills up quickly. Call 433–4658. Rates are: $1/hr, $10/daily maximum.

Privately operated lots across from SEA offer free shuttles to and from the airport. Rates are: $8/daily. Call 433–5308 for current information.

Satellite Transit System

An underground transit system connects the Main Terminal to the North and South Satellite terminals. The South Loop stops at the end of Concourse B and at the South Satellite. The North Loop connects the Main Terminal to the North Satellite and also stops at Concourse C. An underground shuttle in the Main Terminal connects the two loops. The cars run every 2 minutes.

Vans

Van service is available to many points in the Greater Seattle area. Press #46 at one of the courtesy phone centers. Information is available at the Ground Transportation booth.

TRAVELERS SERVICES

Everything from chic to primitive, from stand-up snackbars to elegant restaurants, from art objects to fax machines can be found at SEA. You can have your pet sat, take a shower, or just take it easy in the lounges or waiting areas. SEA's amenities are ample and upscale—among the best at any airport anywhere.

Airline Clubs

Alaska's Board Room	Concourse D.
American's Admiral	Concourse B.
Continental's President	Mezzanine Level, Main Terminal
Delta's Crown	Concourse B.
Northwest's Top Flight	South Satellite.
United's Red Carpet	North Satellite.

(Club International for overseas travelers is located on the Mezzanine level, South Satellite.)

Baggage Storage

Coin lockers are scattered throughout the complex and cost $.75/24 hours.

Ken's Baggage and Storage in the baggage claim area of the Main Terminal is open from 5:30 a.m. to 12:30 a.m, daily. Rates start at $2/day.

Banks

Tele-Trip Currency Exchange is located in all the terminals. Hours are normally 6 a.m. to 9 p.m., daily, but may vary because of international traffic. Call 243–1231.

ATM is in the center of the Main Terminal. American Express Cash Express is near the United counter in the baggage claim area.

Business Services

Pacific Northwest Bell has two business centers, one in the Main Terminal and one in the North Satellite. Individual work stations, copy machines, a fax machine, speaker phones and small conference rooms are available.

Other conference rooms and even an auditorium are available for rent. Call 433–5622.

Cocktail Lounges

Nine lounges are located throughout the complex. Hours are 10 a.m. to 2 a.m.

Gift Shops/Newsstands

Boston has lobster, Seattle is noted for salmon. At the Northwest Shop you can buy fresh salmon plus arts and crafts by regional artists. Comings & Goings is a contemporary sportwear shop. Benjamin Books recently opened a full-line bookstore. All are in the Main Terminal.

Information/Assistance

Up-to-the minute information is available by calling 431–4444, or 1–800–544–1965. The Visitor Information booth, staffed daily 9:30 a.m. to 7:30 p.m., is located in the Baggage Claim area, Main Terminal.
The Travelers Aid desk is staffed daily, 10 a.m. to 10 p.m. It is located on the upper level center of the Main Terminal. Call 433–5288.

Military Services

USO maintains a 24-hour lounge and information referral on the second floor of the Main Terminal. Call 433–5438. For military travel assistance call 281–3095 or 281–3086.

Miscellaneous

Barbershop/shoeshine: Main Terminal, 7 a.m. to 8 p.m., M–F; 9 a.m. to 5 p.m., Sat. Call 248–2969. A shoeshine stand is also in the North Satellite, 6 a.m. to 10 p.m. daily.
Interdenominational Chapel: Main Terminal mezzanine level. Call 433–5505 for times of interdenominational services.
Food storage: Ken's Baggage and Storage, Main Terminal. Frozen food lockers start at $5/24 hrs.
Nursery: Cribs, chairs, and couches are available in the nursery on the ticketing level of the Main Terminal. Changing rooms are located in restrooms throughout the airport.
Pet sitting: Ken's Baggage and Storage, Main Terminal. A 6-pound Pomeranian will cost $1/hr.
Showers: $5. Located at the barbershop in the Main Terminal.

Post

Mail drops and stamp vending are located throughout the complex.

Restaurants/Snack Bars

The Carvery (433–5622) is an elegant dining restaurant located in the center of the Main Terminal. Open 7 a.m. to 10 p.m. daily. A prime rib dinner costs $15.50, but the have-it-your-way salmon at $11.50 is our preference. There is also a 24-hour cafeteria, the French Express, nearby.

TIME TO KILL . . .

1 hour . . . The Pacific Rim cultural exhibit between Concourses C and D is an open-area display tracing the heritage of the Northwest. You can easily while away an hour learning about potlatch, a radical native American share-the-wealth concept.

2 hours. . . . If the weather is pleasant, Salt Water State Park is only about a five-minute bus ride from SEA. Spend a pleasant hour or so far from the maddening crowds and ramble along Puget Sound.

3 hours . . . The Space Needle is practically synonymous with Seattle and worth the trip if you have a long enough layover. Open daily, 9 a.m. to midnight, admission is $3.75. The observation deck is 520 feet above Seattle. The Space Needle Restaurant is moderately priced; the Emerald Suite has a dress requirement. Take the Grey Line Express to Westin Hotel, then catch the monorail ($.60).

4 hours . . . The Pike Place Market is the nation's oldest continuously operating market, a going concern since 1907. A five-story, three-block long structure, the Market has everything from specialty shops to old-fashioned ice cream parlors. Open daily, 9 a.m. to 9 p.m.

For additional information, call the Seattle–King County Convention and Visitors Center, (206) 433–5218.

TAMPA

TAMPA INTERNATIONAL AIRPORT

We like Tampa International. And we're not the only ones. The International Foundation of Airline Passengers Association voted TPA #2 (behind Singapore and tied with Amsterdam) in a poll of 30,000 frequent flyers. Resembling a spoked wheel with its airsides connected to the main terminal by automated shuttle trains, TPA is efficient but relaxed and almost charming.

The Tampa/St. Petersburg metro area is the largest in Florida with over 1.9 million residents, ranking it 21st in the U.S. TPA's growth, though, has been slowed by its proximity to Orlando International.

The first, very first regularly scheduled air services began in Tampa. Aviation pioneer Tony Jannus ran three round-trips daily from Tampa to St. Petersburg beginning Jan. 1, 1914. TPA was the first to install the now standard people-mover trainway in 1971.

QUICK CONTACTS

Medical . . . 911
Police . . . 911
Lost & Found . . . 276–3421
Information . . . 276–3400
Paging . . . Airlines

THE BASICS

Name: Tampa International Airport
Airport Code: TPA
Location: 3 miles northwest of Tampa

Mailing Address: PO Box 22287
            Tampa, FL 33622
Telephone: (813) 276–3400
Time: Eastern
Daily Passengers (Rank): 26,566 (41)
Supervising Body: Hillsborough County Aviation
                 Authority

AIRLINE	TELEPHONE	AIRSIDE
Air Canada	276–3570	C
Air Jamaica	276–3614	F
Air New Orleans	276–3737	B
American	276–3826	F
Bahamas Air	276–3855	E
British Airways	276–3692	F
Cayman Airways	276–3631	F
Continental	276–3871	E
Continental Express	276–3737	B
Delta	276–3320	C
Eastern	878–5916	B
Eastern Express	276–3383	B
Midway	276–3803	E
Northwest	276–3220	D
PanAm	276–3124	E
Piedmont	276–3580	F
Servair	276–3692	D
TWA	276–3240	C
United	276–3263	D
USAir	276–3792	F
Wardair Canada	276–3850	F

FINDING YOUR WAY AROUND

Elevated, automatic trains connect airside buildings
with the Main Terminal. Each Airside (don't look for
Airside A—there isn't one) has basic amenities;
Airside F is the International Terminal and houses
Customs/Immigration. The Main Terminal has three
levels: Ground Transportation and Baggage Claims on
the lower, Ticketing on Level 2, and shops and
restaurants on Level 3. Terminal to Airside trains run
from Level 3. A mini-mall of shops connects Level 3
with the Marriott Hotel. Spacious but not cavernous,
TPA has good signage and plenty of lounging areas.

Over 100 white paging response and emergency phones are located on pillars in key passageways.

INFORMATION FOR THE HANDICAPPED

TPA provides facilities for handicapped and elderly travelers in accordance with Architectural and Transportation Barriers Compliance Board standards. Air travelers are advised to consult with their airline for special needs.

GROUND TRANSPORTATION

Ground Transportation quadrants are located at both ends of Level 1. Tampa lacks Rapid Transit, so there is no fast and cheap transportation to downtown. HART buses run frequently but if you're in a hurry a taxi is your best bet.

Buses

HART provides downtown service approximately every 25 minutes. Fare is 60 cents, and you need exact change. Stop is at east end of Red Flight Departure Drive, Level 2. Call 254–4278.

Car Rentals

Rental counters are located in Baggage Claim Area, Level 1.

Avis	276–3500	Hertz	874–3232
Budget	874–6051	National	276–3782
Dollar	276–3640		

Hotel Shuttles

Two banks of courtesy phones are located in the Baggage Claim Area, Level 1.

Taxis/Limos

All pick-ups are from the Ground Transport Quadrant, Level 1. Average fare to downtown is $13.

Tampa Yellow	253–0121	United	253–2424

Three limo firms serve TPA:

Central Florida Limo	1–665–8157
The Limo	1–822–3333
Pasco Limo	1–847–6161

Parking

TPA can park 4,000 cars in its garage; 1,000 in its open lot.

Terminal garage: $.50/half-hr., $7/daily max.

Open lot: $.50/half hr., $5/daily max.

For parking information, call 276-3690. Radio 1610 AM broadcasts parking information.

TRAVELERS SERVICES

TPA clusters shops in the center of the Main Terminal, Level 3, and then runs a mini-mall toward the Marriott. Most stores are open until 11 p.m., daily. You'll find most of the basic travel needs in these stores, although TPA is probably the only airport where you can buy 100-year-old cigar-making molds.

Airline Clubs

Delta's Crown	Airside C.
Eastern's Ionosphere	Main Terminal, Level 3 (near Airside B)
Piedmont's Presidential	Main Terminal, Level 3 (near Airside B)
SAS	Main Terminal, Level 3 (near Airside B)

Baggage Storage

Coin lockers only. $1/24 hrs.

Banks

NCNB: Main Terminal, Level 3 Mall, Hours: M–Th, 9 a.m. to 4 p.m.; F, 9 a.m. to 6 p.m.

Tele-Trip Currency Exchange: Main Terminal. M–Sat., 7 a.m. to 6 p.m.

One Automatic Teller Machine is located in the Mall area.

Business Services

No centralized facility currently operates. Marriott has fax and copying available for a fee. The hotel also has meeting rooms available. Rates start at $50. Call the Marriott sales office, 879–5151.

Cocktail Lounges

Each Airside has a lounge, plus there are three in the Main Terminal on Level 3. The Flight Room in the Marriott is open until 1 a.m. and overlooks the pool area. The Veranda Bar attracts a livelier crowd, but the Tony Jannus Lounge offers a better view. A popular drink is a triple-shot concoction called the "Blitz," and it will leave you just that.

Gift Shops/Newsstands

Shops offer everything from Florida souvenirs to art and antiques. If you like chocolate you'll love Aiello's where you can buy (for $14.95) an eight-slice chocolate pizza. Monocle Book Store in the Mall area is open daily from 7 a.m. to 10 p.m.

Hotel

Marriott Airport Inn is on-site. Weekday rates start at $118; various weekend packages are available. Call 879–5151.

Information/Assistance

Guide stations are at the top of each escalator in the Main Terminal. Travelers Aid is in the Main Terminal, Level 3. Staffed 9 a.m. to 9 p.m., daily. Call 276–3583.

Miscellaneous

Barber Shop: Level 3, Main Terminal, M–Sat, 7 a.m. to 7 p.m.
Nursery changing: Level 3, Main Terminal.
Shoeshine: Level 3, Main Terminal, M–F, 5 a.m. to 7 p.m., S–Sun., 9 a.m. to 5 p.m. A shine runs $2.

Restaurants/Snack Bars

Each airside has a snackbar, but the Main Terminal offers good sit-down choices. The Terrace Buffet has a $3 salad bar; Tampa Bay Wharf features fresh seafood. The ginger peanut chicken dinner at the Jose Gasparilla is $9.25. For dessert amble down to the Vintage Confectionary—a triple-scoop on a waffle cone is $3.60.

Post

Mail drops and stamp vending machines are located in Airsides and in the Main Terminal.

TIME TO KILL

1 hour . . . With two TV lounges, a full-fledged bookstore and some of the best viewing areas at any airport you can while away an hour easily.

2 hours . . . Have lunch, dinner, or just a drink at CK's, the revolving rooftop restaurant atop the Marriott. CK's rotates a full circle every 80 minutes allowing loungers to take in a panorama of TPA and the Tampa Bay area.

3 hours . . . The Tampa Museum (223–8130) has an extensive collection of contemporary American paintings, plus Mediterranean antiquities. Admission is free. Hours: T, Thurs., F: 10 a.m. to 6 p.m.; W: 10 a.m. to 9 p.m.; Sat.: 9 a.m. to 5 p.m.; Sun.: 1 p.m. to 5 p.m. Closed Mondays.

4 hours . . . Harbour Island offers a variety of good restaurants and up-scale shops. Open daily until 9 p.m. Call (813) 229–5330 for special event information. HART bus #30 will get you there in about 40 minutes for 60 cents.

For additional information, call the Visitors Center, 223–1111, or 1–800–826–8358.

WASHINGTON

WASHINGTON DULLES INTERNATIONAL AIRPORT

This airport was opened in 1962 amidst some controversy about its location. It is relatively remote from the Washington D.C. population hub, but the Jet Age required longer runways and more room than was available at National. With 10,000 acres, Dulles has room. On the eve of a $600 million expansion/renovation program (a new international terminal is already underway), Dulles is getting its first major facelift since opening.

The airport was named for John Foster Dulles, Secretary of State during the Eisenhower administration.

You can't see it, but the prototype space shuttle "Enterprise" is stored here along with other military aircraft. The shuttle will be a featured exhibit in a hoped-for Air and Space Museum to be erected on-site if and when funds become available.

QUICK CONTACTS

Medical . . . 661–9211
Police. . . . 471–4114
Lost & Found. . . . 471–4114
Information . . . 471–7838
Paging. . . . Airlines Only

THE BASICS

Name: Washington Dulles International Airport
Airport Codes: IAD
Mailing Address: PO Box 17045
                 Washington, D.C. 20041

Telephone: (202) 471–7838
Location: 26 miles west of Washington, D.C.
Time: Eastern
Daily Passengers (Rank): 29,547 (37)
Supervising Body: Metropolitan Washington Airports
Authority

AIRLINE	TELEPHONE
All airline ticket counters are on the Main Floor.	
Aeroflot	332–1498
Air France	1–800–237–2747
All Nippon	1–800–262–2359
American	393–2345
American Eagle	1–800–552–7802
Braniff	1–800–272–6433
British Airways	393–5300
Continental	1–800–525–0280
Continental Express	631–1933
Delta	468–2282
Eastern	393–4000
Lufthansa	1–800–645–3880
Northwest	737–7333
Pan Am	833–1000
Presidential	478–9700
Republic	1–800–441–1414
TWA	737–7400
United	893–3400
United Express	893–3400
USAir	783–4500
Western Airlines	1–800–227–6105

FINDING YOUR WAY AROUND

It's easy to find your way around this airy, two-story complex. Gate assignments, especially on international flights, change frequently so consult with your carrier for exact departure gates and the locations of the mobile lounges that run to the two mid-field terminals.

INFORMATION FOR THE HANDICAPPED

IAD meets standard provided by the Architectural and Transportation Barriers Compliance Board. A TDD unit is located in the Travelers Aid booth in the Main Terminal. All passengers who may require

WASHINGTON DULLES INTERNATIONAL AIRPORT

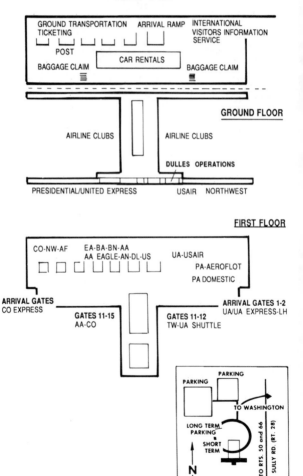

special assistance are advised to notify their carrier prior to departure.

GROUND TRANSPORTATION

All ground transportation departs from the West and East ramps, ground floor. Tickets and schedules are available at information counters adjacent to baggage claim areas.

Buses/Rapid Transit

There is no public bus transport. The Washington Flyer is the primary source of ground transportation, providing extensive service throughout the D.C. Metro area. Flyers run every 30 minutes from 6:15 a.m. to 1:15 a.m. Fare to downtown D.C. is $12, $20 round-trip. Call (703) 685–1400. The Flyer also provides service to the West Falls Church Metrorail Station. Coaches leave every 45 minutes. The 20-minute trip costs $5 one-way, $9 roundtrip. Metrorail Rapid Transit to Capitol Mall is $2.40 ($1.10 off-peak hours).

Car Rentals

Rental cars are available 24 hours a day. Counters are located in the Main Terminal, ground floor.

Avis	1–800–331–1212	Hertz	1–800–654–3131
Budget	1–800–527–0700	National	1–800–328–4567
Dollar	1–800–421–6868		

Hotel Shuttles

Hotel courtesy phones are located on the Main Terminal ground floor, adjacent to the rental car counters.

Taxis/Limos

Taxi dispatchers are on duty 24 hours. Call (202) 471–5555. Fare to downtown D.C. is $25.
Dafre Inc provides limo service. For information call 690–3102, or 685–1400.

Parking

Continuous shuttle buses provide free transportation to the terminal from satellite lots. Short term parking:

$1.50/hr; $18/daily maximum. Daily parking $1/hr, $6/daily maximum. Long term satellite lots, $3/daily. Parking for the handicapped is in the hourly lot adjacent to the terminal.

TRAVELERS SERVICES

Amenities are primarily clustered on the main floor of the terminal. You'll find the basic services and eateries, however, throughout the complex.

Airline Clubs

All Nippon Air	South Finger
American's Admiral	Concourse D
British Airways	Western end, Main Floor
Continental's President's	Concourse D
Lufthansa	South Finger
Pan American's Clipper	South Finger
TWA's Ambassador	South Finger

Baggage Storage

Coin lockers are located at the entrance of the South Finger, Ground Floor. $1/24 hours.

Business Services

Mutual of Omaha Tele-Trip Travelers Service centers are located in the east and west end of the Main Terminal. Services include copying, fax, notary. Open daily, 7 a.m. to 10 p.m. Call 661–8864.

Banks

Sovereign Bank is located on the ground floor of the Main Terminal. Hours: M–F, 9 a.m. to 1 p.m.; 3 p.m. to 5 p.m. Call 471–7498.
American Express is located on the Ground Floor, east end, Main Terminal.

Cocktail Lounges

There are seven lounges scattered throughout the complex. The one on the Main Floor of the Main Terminal is open until midnight.

Gift Shops/Newsstands

Gift shops are on the main floor. They are open to 11 p.m. daily.

Newsstands are located throughout the complex. The newsstand on the main floor, west end, is open 24 hours.

Information/Assistance

The information booth is located on the ground floor of the Main Terminal. Open M–F, 8:30 a.m. to 5 p.m. Call 471–7838. Travelers Aid is located on the ground floor of the Main Terminal, west end. Hours: Sun–F, 10 a.m. to 9 p.m.; Sat, 10 a.m. to 6 p.m. Call 661–8636.

The International Information Booth, Language Assistance, is located on the ground floor, Main Terminal. Open daily, noon to 7 p.m.

Miscellaneous Services

Barbershop: east end, main floor. Open M–F, 9 a.m. to 6 p.m.

Bookstore: east end, main floor. Hours are daily, 7 a.m. to 10 p.m.

Restaurants/Snack Bars

The Diplomat, a full-service restaurant, is located on the main floor of the Main Terminal. It is open 7 a.m. to 9 p.m., daily.

Snack bars abound (there are 6 total). The one in the Main Terminal, main floor, is open 24 hours.

Post

A full-service post office is located at the west end, ground floor of the Main Terminal. Hours: M–F, 8:30 a.m. to 4 p.m. Mail drops and vending machines are scattered throughout the complex.

TIME TO KILL

IAD's distance from D.C. (26 miles) and lack of easy access to Rapid Transit makes venturing off the grounds time consuming. You need to allow at least 2 hours just for round trip transportation to D.C.

3 hours . . . Reston is five miles away. A planned community in its 26th year, this city of 52,000 is a trendy residential area. It's the type of town where you can get emergency brain surgery but not your yard mowed. Notice the absence of sidewalks. Call the Reston Visitors Information Center, (703) 471–7030.

4 hours . . . Up North they know it as Manassas, in the old Cotton Kingdom it's Bull Run. The battlefield is 15 miles south of Dulles. During spring and summer reenactments of battle incidents are common. The museum is open daily, 8:30 a.m. to 5 p.m. Admission is $1. For more information, call (703) 754–7107.

If you have more time and want to journey into D.C. call the D.C. Visitor Information Center, (202) 789–7000.

WASHINGTON

WASHINGTON NATIONAL INTERNATIONAL AIRPORT

This is the nation's first federally owned airport, dedicated in 1941 (the cornerstone was laid by Franklin D. Roosevelt), and it's due for a facelift. Approximately $400 million will be used to give National its first major overhaul since its opening.

With only 680 acres, National is the smallest "major" airport in the US.

Despite its "International" designation, National deplanes no international passengers.

QUICK CONTACTS

Medical. . . . 557–2111
Police. . . . 557–2581
Lost & Found. . . . 557–2619
Information . . . 685–8000
Paging. . . . Airlines

THE BASICS

Name: Washington National International Airport
Airport Code: DCA
Mailing address: Washington National Airport
                Washington, D.C. 20001
Telephone: (703) 685–8000
Location: 4 miles south of Washington, D.C.
Time: Eastern
Daily Passengers (Rank): 42,301 (25)
Supervising Body: Metropolitan Washington Airports
                Authority

AIRLINE	TELEPHONE	TERMINAL
American Airlines	393–2345	American
Braniff	1–800–527–5158	Main
Continental	1–800–525–0280	American
Delta	301–468–2282	North
Eastern	393–4000	Main
Jet America	1–800–421–7574	American
Midway	1–800–621–5700	NW/TWA
Midwest Express	1–800–452–2022	Main
Northwest	737–7333	NW/TWA
Pan Am	833–1000	North
Piedmont	703–620–0400	Piedmont
TWA	737–7400	NW/TWA
United	703–893–3400	Main
USAir	783–4500	Main
Western Air	1–800–227–6105	American

FINDING YOUR WAY AROUND

The Main Terminal is a curving, two-level structure. Walking from Gate 1 in the Northwest/TWA Terminal to Gate 42 in the North Terminal takes about 10 minutes. There are no moving sidewalks or automated trains. DCA is the way airline terminals used to look.

INFORMATION FOR THE HANDICAPPED

DCA provides facilities for handicapped and elderly travelers in accordance with standards of the Architectural and Transportation Barriers Compliance Board. A specially equipped van is available free of charge for transportation to any point on the airport. A TDD phone unit is located at the Travelers Aid booth in the Main Terminal.

GROUND TRANSPORTATION

As befitting the nation's capital, National has various modes of transportation which serve D.C. and the surrounding areas. Metrorail is the most popular.

Buses/Rapid Transit

The Metrorail station is located opposite the North Terminal. The trains leave every 10 minutes; fare is $.80 for the 15 minute trip to the Capitol Mall area.

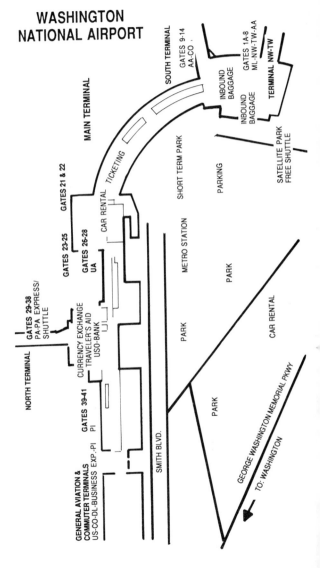

WASHINGTON NATIONAL AIRPORT

WASHINGTON D.C.

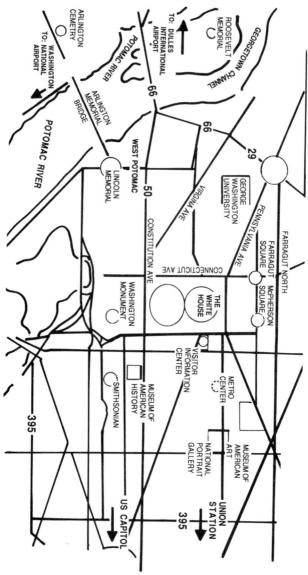

Trains operate M–F, 5:30 a.m. until midnight; Sat,
8 a.m. to midnight; Sun, 10 a.m. to midnight. For
information call 637–2000. There are no public buses.

Car Rentals

Counters are located in all terminals. They are open
until 11 p.m., daily.

Avis	739–4810	Hertz	471–6020
Budget	800–527–0700	National	783–1590
Dollar	800–421–6868		

Hotel Shuttles

Hotel courtesy phones are located in the Main
Terminal, south area.

Motor Coach Service

The Washington Flyer is the primary service. Flyers
run every 30 minutes to D.C. and outlying areas. Fare
is $5 one-way, $8 round-trip. The Flyer operates until
10 p.m. For information call 685–1400.
Groome Transportation also provides motor coach
service to Richmond and Fredericksburg. Call (202)
587–7629.

Taxis

Taxis are available in front of the terminals. The rate
to downtown D.C. is approximately $8.

Parking

Short term rates are $2/hr, $20/daily maximum. Lots
1,2, and 3: $1.50/hr, $7.50/daily maximum. Satellites
are $.75/hr, $6/daily maximum.
Free shuttle buses connect terminals with lots 2 and 3,
and satellites A and B.
For parking information call 684–7766, or tune your
radio to 530 AM.

TRAVELERS SERVICES

DCA's amenities are unvarnished. Saunas and
sleepers won't be found, but you can grab a
newspaper, get a bite to eat, or a shoeshine.

Airline Clubs

American's Admiral	Main Terminal
Eastern's Ionosphere	Main Terminal, second floor
Northwest's Top Flight	NW/TWA Terminal
Pan Am's Clipper	North Terminal
Piedmont's Presidential	North Terminal, upper level
TWA's Ambassador	NW/TWA Terminal
United's Red Carpet	North Concourse
USAir's Club	Main Terminal

Baggage Storage

Lockers are located behind the security checkpoints. Rate: $.75/24 hrs.

Banks

First American Bank of Virginia, Room 274 upper level of main terminal. Hours: M–Th, 9 a.m. to 2 p.m.; F, 9 a.m. to 2 p.m., 3 p.m. to 7 p.m.; Sat, 9 a.m. to noon. Call 827–8525.

There are 2 American Express ATMs: one on the North Concourse adjacent to the United Airlines gate, and the other in the Main Terminal near the Eastern Shuttle counter. The only ATM is also near the Eastern Shuttle gate.

Tele-Trip Currency Exchange is in the Main lobby, and also in the entryway to the NW/TW Terminal. Call 979–8383.

Business Services

Tele-Trip Travelers Services offers copying, faxing, Telex/telegram, notary. Open daily, 6 a.m. to 10 p.m. Located in the main level of the Main Terminal. Call 979–8383.

Cocktail Lounges

There are three cocktail lounges. The one in the Main Terminal lobby is open until 10 p.m., daily. The two others, in Main Terminal South and in the North Terminal, are open until 11 p.m., daily.

Gift Shops/Newsstands

Two gift shops are located in the Main Terminal lobby and on the South Concourse. Open daily, 7 a.m. to 11 p.m. Newsstand hours vary, but the one in the lobby is open 24 hours.

Information/Assistance

An information booth is located in the Main Terminal. Open daily, 7 a.m. to 10 p.m. Call 685–8000. Travelers Aid is located in the Main Terminal. Open daily, 9 a.m. to 9 p.m. Call 683–3472.

Military Services

The USO information booth is located in the North Terminal. Call 920–2705. The USO lounge is located on the North Concourse. Call 920–6990.

Miscellaneous Services

Barbershop: Main Terminal, open daily, 8 a.m. to 8 p.m.

Post

A full service post office is located in the Main Terminal South. Hours: M–F, 8:30 a.m. to 5 p.m.; Sat, 8:30 a.m. to noon. Mail drops are located throughout the complex.

Restaurants/Snack Bars

A full-service restaurant is located in the main lobby of the Main Terminal. Open M–Th, Sat.–Sun. 7 a.m. to 9 p.m., Friday 7 a.m. to 8 p.m.
The "buffeteria" in Main Terminal south is open 24 hours.
Four other eateries are scattered throughout the complex.

TIME TO KILL

1 Hour . . . Arlington National Cemetery is less than 10 minutes by Blue Line Metrorail. Open 8 a.m. to 5 p.m., daily. Changing of the guard at the

Tomb of the Unknown Soldier happens hourly on the hour. Admission is free. The Iwo Jima Memorial is about a five-minute walk.

2 Hours . . . or 3 Hours . . . or 4 Hours . . .

Take the Yellow Metrorail and in 15 minutes you're in the Capitol Mall area. Our recommendation begins with the Smithsonian, any one of the museums, and ends with the Smithsonian. Start with the American History Museum at Constitution and 14th Avenue. All are open daily, 10 a.m. to 5 p.m. Admission is free.

For additional information, call the Visitor Information Center (202) 789–7000.

Passenger Rights:

Avoiding Terminal Trauma

Traveler's Nightmare:

You're stuck in ATL (Atlanta) with baggage in MEM (Memphis), a major client awaiting your arrival any minute in DEN (Denver) and your ticket is in your briefcase on its way to MIA (Miami). What, you ask yourself, did I do to deserve this mess?

We strongly believe most problems can be avoided, that those who are prepared will least likely find themselves aloft lacking aerodynamic stability. To wit:

BEFORE YOU LEAVE

A) The TICKET—Make sure your travel agent or the airline reservationist has all the little details straight, i.e., flight number, times, gate numbers, seat numbers—even that your name is spelled correctly or at least matches what's on your driver's license. And don't lose your ticket. A ticket is almost as negotiable as currency and any finder can use it. (Think about it—when was the last time your ID was checked when you boarded a plane). Jot down the ticket number and put it in your wallet.

B) PACKING—Contrary to popular belief, leaving all those tags flag you as a novice. Experienced travelers know they can sometimes confuse luggage sorters. The only thing you want on the outside of your luggage is your name, address, phone number, and the tag for where it's going THIS trip. As for packing, if you insist on wrapping a Faberge egg in tissue then you deserve to have it broken. Finally, take about 60 seconds and inventory. Leave the list at home or with somebody you can contact quickly—secretary, spouse, or girlfriend/boyfriend. Once in a while, luggage is lost or stolen and you'd be surprised at how many folks don't have the foggiest idea of what was in there.

C) CONFIRM FLIGHT DEPARTURE—It may seem like an unnecessary exercise, but when your teenager drops you off at the airport like a hot potato and you find airline personnel are conspicuously scarce—you know your flight has been delayed and you should have called.

SNAFUS

LOST TICKET—We can't believe you did this. Don't panic, just dash to the appropriate airline counter and report your ticket number. You did write it down, didn't you? You'll get a refund provided that the finder did not use the ticket. But be aware that you will pay a penalty for your carelessness.

DELAYED LUGGAGE—This is the state of luggage limbo. While you are glued to Carousel B in Newark your luggage is traveling around the U.S. racking up mileage points. Ho hum, you say, you didn't need a change of underwear for tomorrow's regional meeting anyway. Don't worry. Although airlines don't advertise it and some are more generous than others, a fair reparation is available. But be reasonable—don't demand Brooks Brothers or Evan-Picone. If you need certain items, say so. Most airlines will accommodate.

LOST OR DAMAGED BAGGAGE—This really doesn't happen often but, like breaking a leg, it only has to happen once for you to feel the pain. Make sure you have a list of what's in your luggage and please, no valuables. Keep Aunt Bette's antique brooch with you. OK, the hard, cold facts. If your luggage is assumed lost on a domestic flight—the maximum the airlines have to fork over is $1,250 per

person.* You also have to prove your loss and you are
not going to like this part—the airlines will pay
depreciated value only. File a formal claim before you
leave the airport and have that inventory list handy—
it will make your argument stronger.

If you have been on an international flight, the
Warsaw Convention takes over. Repayment is based
on kilos converted into pounds × francs converted to
dollars (did we lose you?). Roughly calculated, if your
bags weighed 50 lbs., at the present rate of exchange
you'd get approximately $450. Not very good.

As for damaged luggage, if it can be repaired, the
airline will usually pay for the repairs. But, if it is
unrecognizable then the airline will negotiate a
settlement based on its depreciated value.

Remember the Faberge egg? Airlines generally will
not compensate you for damaged property inside
your luggage unless there is evidence of external
damage to the luggage.

DELAYED FLIGHTS—If the problem is weather,
there is not much you can do. On the other hand, if it
is mechanical or a delayed incoming flight, ask if you
can change flights or even airlines. Often the carrier
that issued your ticket will endorse it to another
airline. Be sure that you are not charged a penalty or a
higher fare. If you find yourself stranded, check with
airline personnel to elicit what services they will
provide. Or, find a quiet corner, prop up your feet
and read our book.

CANCELLED FLIGHTS—Back when airlines were
booking flights right up to bankruptcy filings this was
a problem. Wholesale cancellations now are rare.
Generally when it does happen the airline will re-

* You can obtain additional baggage coverage from
some airlines or at many airport insurance counters.
Consider doing it. Two business suits, some dress
shirts, shoes, etc., can easily run over the $1,250
ceiling.

schedule you on the first available flight. As in a
delayed flight, promptly interrogate airline personnel
and find out what you can extract from them for this
inconvenience.

OVERBOOKING—We need to discuss VBs
(Voluntary Bumpings) and IBs (Involuntary
Bumpings). Or as one acquaintance of ours refers to
it—PBs (for "Pay Backs"). Overbookings are
becoming less common as the airlines have gone to
super-sophisticated computer systems that allow
them to predict with actuarial precision how many
passengers will board a given flight. (If they can do
that, why are they always short pillows and
blankets?) Still, you may be a victim of this
occurrence and you need to know what you are
entitled to.

VB—Voluntary Bumping. When an airline has
overbooked a flight, it must call for volunteers to
sacrifice their seats. Since it is unnatural to volunteer
(remember your Army days) you may be hesitant.
We're not going to tell you to raise your hand, but we
are going to suggest you consider it. For example, if
you can catch another flight in a reasonable amount of
time (your decision) and you want to try your hand at
the wheel of fortune, step forward. The airlines will
offer either money, a free ticket or other benefits. Our
recommendation: take the ticket.

IB—Involuntary Bumping. This gets tricky: the U.S.
Department of Transportation has some decided rules
on involuntary bumping.

If you're IBed and the airline can arrange substitute
transportation (no camels, skateboards or kayaks) that
puts you where you're supposed to be within one
hour of your original arrival time, you're entitled to
nothing. No free tickets, no money, no meals. You can
bet the airlines have a pretty good handle on who
they can bump and re-schedule with little cost to
them.

However, if the alternate air arrangement gets you
home more than one hour and less than two hours

after your original arrival time, you are entitled to a bonus equivalent to the one-way fare to your final destination, but not to exceed $200.

If the substitute transportation goes over two hours delay, or the airline does not make arrangements for you, the compensation doubles but may not exceed $400.

The Fine Print: You are not entitled to compensation if:

a) You are late for check-in. Time requirements will differ from airline to airline and check-in deadline can vary from 10 minutes to 90 and from flight to flight. Always, always, *always* honor the check-in deadline.

b) The flight is cancelled or is an international flight.

c) Your aircraft had a seating capacity of 60 or less.

A Fine Point: Although air travel is up, the problems of overbookings are going down. Industry-wide figures as compiled by the D.O.T. reflect a rate of a little more than 3 bumpings for every 10,000 boardings. For example, in the first six months of 1988, American Airlines had 47,000 voluntary bumpings and only 164 involuntary bumpings. When you consider its boardings of 30.6 million you can understand that the likelihood of being bumped is minimal.

CONSTRUCTIVE COMPLAINING—True story: An irate passenger took a major airline to court because the film projector on the cross-country flight broke and he could not watch the movie. He wanted a refund of his fare. The airline offered a pre-trial settlement of a movie ticket. Everyone got a good laugh except the plaintiff. The judge awarded him nothing.

There is an art to obtaining redress for your wrongs. In the airline industry, procedures are to be followed—both written and otherwise—if you want action.

a) Start with the airline. If you feel wronged, immediately ask to see a Customer Service Representative. All airlines have troubleshooters with the authority to settle problems on the spot. State your case, what you want and why, and let them make the next move. You'll probably end up with a compromise but sometimes a speedy settlement is better than pursuing a complaint for the rest of your natural life.

b) If you are not satisfied with what the airport airline personnel offer and want to continue, then:

> Type a letter to the airline's consumer office and include a precise description of your complaint. If a certain flight is involved, be specific. Don't say: "On your Friday flight from DFW to DTW . . ." but rather: "On Flight #123, Friday, Dec. 17, from Dallas to Detroit . . ." Make sure you include an address and phone number.

> Be cool and assertive. Don't get hysterical and don't make ridiculous demands. Insisting that the entire crew be fired because you didn't get a window seat immediately marks you as a crank.

> OK, you got nowhere with the airlines and you are spitting fire. What is left? You can file a complaint about the airline with the Department of Transportation (D.O.T.)

Write: Office of Community and Consumers Affairs
          U.S. Department of Transportation
          400 7th Street, S.W.
          Room 10405
          Washington, D.C. 20590

Or call: (202) 366–2220.
And for the record. . . . the D.O.T. publishes an insightful guide titled, "FLY-RIGHTS" It is free.

Write: U.S. Department of Transportation
          Office of the Secretary of Transportation
          400 7th St. SW
          Washington, DC 20590

FINALLY—You did all of the above and things still didn't go right. You must face the possibility that *you* screwed up and that there is no one to blame but yourself. We've had some experience in this and we have found that airline personnel can sometimes perform miracles. A lot depends on your attitude.

When things are really rough get down on your knees, beg for forgiveness, promise to pay college tuition or name your first born after them (Do you suppose Delta Burke got her name this way?). It might work.

NOTES

NOTES